Don't Fault the Moon

A Daughter's Reflections

A Memoir

Nancy Hill

To my family... with love to the moon and back.

Table of Contents

INTRODUCTION

I like to say I come from a long line of writers . . . but when I do, I hope no one asks me, "How long?"

In truth, not so long.

My father, Kermit Hill, was a writer, as was his father before him. My grandfather, Clarence, worked as a self-taught newspaperman in several small, backwoods towns in Kansas and Arkansas. These jobs eventually led him to Kansas City, Missouri, and employment as a reporter with the *Kansas City Star*. There, in the late 1930s, he was promoted to the position of church column editor. His son, my father, grew up immersed in journalism, where he acquired an appetite for the business and the craft of writing.

I don't know if the Hill family writing gene dates back further than Clarence, but I know I owe some of my passion for writing to my father, Kermit. That is, the man who was my father until I was ten — when he became my absent, ex-father. Like his father, he too became a newspaperman and editor. And, eventually, an author. At age 79, Kermit wrote and self-published an autobiography called *Those Were the Days*. Shortly thereafter, he penned a fictional, semi-autobiographical novel about a news reporter called *Brad*. Although neither book, in my opinion, was of publication quality, the books exist in print today — they can be held, touched, scanned, scoured, accepted, rejected, shelved.

Perhaps because Kermit chose not to include me as a character in his life story, I am determined to prove something. If that father, such as he was, could publish two books, then surely I can produce at least one. It is time. With a clenched jaw, I say to my now-deceased father, this one — your daughter's memoir — is for you.

The author, Toni Morrison, is reported to have said, "If there is a book that you want to read, but it hasn't been written yet, you must be the one to write it." This statement rings in my ears as I find myself with a story to tell.

I humbly call myself a writer. One who has, from high school to college and throughout a career as an educator, met ongoing demands for written product. Who has, over the years, excelled in writing, both personally and professionally. Who is regularly complimented on her written work. Such kudos charge my literary batteries.

In retirement, no longer required to write, I joined writing classes and groups where I began to pen my long-envisioned memoir. Still in my mind's eye are Emma Krumseik and Robert McGhee of the formidable English Department at my high school in Raytown, Missouri; even now, I draw upon their confidence in my literary promise.

And I think back to a year when I, myself a principal, imparted "words of wisdom" to a remarkable class of graduating sixth graders. I spoke of goals and asked each of those promising students, as they headed to junior high school, to identify a goal and be determined to achieve it. That day, for the first time in public, I announced my own goal—to write a book. I guaranteed my students that I would do it. That promise is almost thirty years old. It's time, dear students. This one's for you.

So how did my idea begin? Was it conceived unwittingly in a high school composition class with that demanding teacher, Miss Krumseik—the feared honors teacher, referred to as "battle-ax" by some of her less-than-literary charges? Who never let even one student off the hook? Who inspired not with warm validation but with iron-fisted determination? Who deigned to wring the best of thoughts from each student's reluctant seventeen-year-old brain? Who saw to it that such thoughts translated to errorless, if naïve, sentences and paragraphs?

Or did my story begin in another high school class as I raptured to my literature teacher's daily recitations of famed passages? As that lofty teacher-bard, Mr. McGhee—undeterred by the snickers of his less inspired young charges—led us through centuries and decades of writings, subliminally inspiring my own virginal pages?

Were the seeds of my memoir fertilized in college writing classes, even when the chief activity was watching the professor light and relight his pipe? Did the required readings in undergraduate literature classes provide fodder for my own tender syllables striving to germinate? Could this take over fifty years?

To all of the above, I think yes. But it still may leave you to wonder why a completely ordinary person like me would presume to produce a memoir. I am not famous, not a celebrity (whose memoirs, as you know, top the current best-seller lists). My story is no more remarkable than that of any other person who was once a child, who survived a family. Surely a memoir resides in the heart of everyone who has lived for even part of a lifetime. Those stories, if put to writing, would be compelling, wise, witty, profound, fun . . . at least as memorable as mine.

But still I write . . . in vindication, and to keep a promise.

And there is yet another motivator—one which harks back to a hilarious evening long ago when I and my then-dearest friend, Emilie, were left to our own devices by our traveling husbands. Over the years, Emilie—a world-class listener—had heard the tales of my tortured youth and fractured family. Amid peals of laughter or spasms of tears, as my personal writing cheerleader, she demanded that I write a book. That evening, Emilie pulled out a notebook . . . and a second bottle of wine.

"It's time to get started." Her words slurred slightly. "I will interview you."

There followed a barrage of questions upon which I was only too happy to expound. Emilie took furious notes. Our session lasted into the wee hours. There was a lot of material. There was a lot of wine.

In the harsh light of the next day, Emilie and I dismayed. The copious notes of the compelling interview were no more legible than the scratchings of a chicken. Page after frazzled page, not a word could be deciphered.

This debacle happened thirty years ago. Time passed. Both Emilie and I moved away. Sadly, we lost touch, for almost twenty years. And then, as life would have it, framed by serendipity and sunset, Emilie reappeared in my life. Ours was a completely unexpected encounter on a golden Florida shoreline among mutual friends. Without missing a beat, Emilie and I rekindled our friendship. I told her that my book was finally in progress. That, over the last year, I had penned almost half of the story she had found so compelling some thirty years ago.

"Oh, Nancy, really? You mean THE book . . . the one I said you *had* to write?"

"Yes, Em. THE book. You were my muse!"

Now two giddy septuagenarians, we relived the night of the famed, failed interview. Again we shared peals of laughter, wistful tears, wine.

Well, Emilie, it's time. The book is forthcoming. And, together with my other sources of inspiration, this one's for you.

So I say that a memoir begins at the moment one envisions a story to be told. The story can be long or short, complex or simple, ordinary or unique. It can grow from a tiny seed or an overwhelming landslide, or both. Given the right conditions — thought, care, love, support, luck — the seed will germinate. The writer will grow. The story will grow, perhaps into something that can be harvested, shared, and consumed by others. And thus, that seed of a memoir, conceived so long ago, will be written.

5

TRACINGS OF SILVER

"If you cannot get rid of the family skeleton, you may as well make it dance."

George Bernard Shaw

Omega

I answer on the third ring. The receiver cradles my ear like the shell of a conch, spawning a wave that sweeps me to my knees. Within its frosty wake, I perceive a vision of my ten-year-old self. A fearful message engulfs me.

With heart pounding like the surf and eyes wide as the moon at its apex, I turn to my husband and say, "It's over."

Alpha

$\mathcal{T}$hey said I nearly died as an infant. Wouldn't eat; rejected both formula and tea; cried incessantly; became dehydrated, scrawny, pale. There were dire predictions. The oft-repeated tale was rather dramatic: Aunt Julie, my mother's older and only sibling, demanded that Mother whisk me onto a plane straight to Kansas City, the ancestral home, where Julie had old Dr. Culp waiting. The venerable family doctor reportedly saved me with long needles, intravenous fluids and mere moments to spare. It was said that I could tolerate nothing but weak tea for a time.

Over the years, I became skeptical of this account. There were too many unanswered questions:

---Were there truly no competent pediatricians in my birth city of Washington, DC, in 1947?

---Were cross-country flights available, at a moment's notice, with affordable fares for average members of the general public?

---Was my father completely removed from this near-death drama starring his firstborn infant daughter?

---Who, in reality, feeds tea to a newborn?

---And those who know me well would ask, could I ever have been scrawny and pale?

As far as family lore goes, the story stood the test of time. In fact, years later, Aunt Julie claimed that old Dr. Culp had said not to let my mother anywhere near me. She did not elaborate about his intent, but by the time Julie related that part to me, it made sense. Only too well, by then, did I know of my mother's infinitesimal tolerance for trauma. And I had learned from my own experience how unnerving a firstborn child can be, especially one as frightening and frustrating as I was. Over the years, I had long suspected that both Mother and I somehow failed our first, most essential bonding challenge. And, given eventual events, my father's absence in the drama was altogether plausible.

In truth, I never disclosed my skepticism toward this account of my earliest escapade. It fit with what later became my role with my mother . . . and was further confirmed by my father's relationships over time with both of us. Not to mention that, even now, I despise tea.

My mother's name was Violet—beautiful, sad, and shrinking. My father was Kermit, as in The Frog—he had been a frogman in the war. They named me Nancy, perhaps hoping that I, like Frank Sinatra's daughter, would become the embodiment of his song—my mother's favorite— "Nancy With the Laughing Face."

Our family triad generated a tale of life, love,

laughter, loss, survival, and lessons I learned along the way—some I wanted to learn and some I didn't. In retrospect, though, all the lessons were vital—how to look and listen, win and lose, seek and hide, connect and sever— to cope, to reinvent, to survive. And, over a lifetime, to attempt to understand and accept a sometimes funny, often frustrating, seriously fractured and, in the final analysis, nearly fatal family.

ON THE RISE

"Hurt is a great teacher. Maybe the greatest of all."

Pat Conroy

Treat . . . or Trick?

*I*t was Halloween, 1954. (Note—If you are tempted to dismiss this tale as preposterous, keep in mind that "back in the day," such a trick-or-treat scenario, although not commonplace, was indeed possible. This one happens to be quite true.) Picture it:

A darkening evening of Halloweening, temperate for Rochester, New York. A sliver of a moon waxes above the fifteen or twenty identical, two-story red brick apartment buildings of the Strathmore Circle plan. Giddy trick-or-treaters gloat over the contents of their brown grocery-sack treat bags. Decked out in homemade costumes, princesses, ghosts, bats, witches, and cowboys of all sizes rush home to enjoy the fruits of their labors.

Enter two small marauders, unwilling to give up just yet. One last stop for a seven-year-old angel and her ghostly girlfriend . . . a building fairly far from home, but still within the allowable boundaries. Porch lights flick out like waning fireflies as the customary trick-or-treating time draws to a close. The two girls, undeterred, knock with determination at one of the last lighted doorways. The door pops open.

"Ah, look! An angel and a ghost! Step right in. We have a very special treat for you tonight!"

That angel was me. My little ghost friend, whose name is lost in my memory, was complicit in our last-ditch quest for candy. But the boisterous greeting caught us off guard. Momentarily tongue-tied, we exchanged glances out of the corners of our narrowed eyes. Though there was no "stranger danger" mantra in those years, I felt a shiver at being asked inside. We stepped but a foot into the warm, well-lighted apartment, bags outstretched. Hoping, perhaps, for a rare popcorn ball.

The "special treat" was nothing of the kind. I sucked in a sharp breath and gasped when I saw what the smiling man held before our eyes. My friend and I turned to each other with unison shrieks.

"Kittens!" Did our feet leave the floor?

We froze in silence, bags gaping, now rooted to the ground. Trying hard to process the incoming barrage of questions from a woman who stood beside the man.

"How old are you? Do you have any pets? Do you live nearby? Will your parents approve?"

We eyed each other with unspoken collusion and nodded our heads vigorously. In the affirmative. My stomach turned a cartwheel.

"Okay, then. Go straight home. And, just in case your parents say no, we will leave our light on for an hour. You can return your kitten by nine o'clock. After that, it'll be yours." He flashed us a serious look. "Remember…no returns after that. Happy Halloween!"

The man placed the kittens with care on top of our collection of treats. The big brown bags crunched and wiggled. Resisting the urge to take the furball out and cuddle him to my chest, I sucked in my breath as if preparing for a marathon. A race whose trophy would be this object of my instant affection. Already I was in love, prepared to lay down my life for that precious prize.

To say that we flew home would be an understatement. The buildings of Strathmore Circle blurred as our fleet little feet grazed the pavement from one corner to the next. After many blocks and only a few wrong turns, we reached our street. We had no time or extra breath for goodbyes.

Inside my building, I flew up two flights of stairs, conjuring a fleeting vision of a shocked mother and a red-faced father.

Bursting through the door, I came up short, nearly overrunning my parents on the couch. Rapid heartbeats pounded in my ears.

"Guess what I got? But . . . but . . . we CAN take him back if we need to. But . . . but . . . it has to be before nine o'clock."

My words escaped without forethought or cunning. They just blurted right out. My blindsided father crumpled his newspaper and bounded toward me.

"Him WHO?" He gaped into the bag. His hand shot out, upending everything. "What the hell? A kitten!"

No doubt frightened by the fracas, the little bundle

leapt away and skittered to the kitchen in a frenzied flurry of gray fur.

"You absolutely WILL take him back! Who in God's name gives a second-grader a cat in their Halloween bag? Find that animal right now!"

My frazzled mother dashed into the small kitchen as the 9:00 p.m. deadline loomed. The kitten was nowhere to be seen. We surmised that he tucked himself among the pipes behind our free-standing stove—cozy, unreachable. *Stay hidden, sweet kitten*, I prayed.

The deadline passed that night and once again the next evening. But, at last, a tentative gray shadow crept out, enticed by furtive tidbits of kibble. In the meantime, despite ongoing interrogation, nothing had surfaced regarding the apartment building from which the preposterous Halloween treat originated. My own memories had disappeared like a puff of smoke, and mum was the word throughout the neighborhood.

With undaunted hope, and with Mother as my conspirator, I conducted a relentless campaign.

"Can we please keep him? Please, please?" I bit my fingernails to the quick.

Though not known to suffer defeat, my father, Kermit, finally gave up. We named the furry gray critter Smokey. He had found a forever home at 20 Strathmore Circle. Our family knew nothing about cats and had never entertained having one, but even Kermit acknowledged that Smokey was a cutie. I had a pet!

I have no recollection of what ever happened to my friend and her own happy Halloween prize.

Two months later, a merry fir tree rose in the living room. Fluffy, fat snowflakes descended outside, and colorful lights bloomed within. Kermit unpacked his favorite Christmas accessory and snapped the rails into place around the base of the tree. A Lionel train began its holiday rounds to the delight of all, especially Smokey—who skillfully batted the little cars off the tracks and across the room. Everyone took turns restraining the kitten in order to save the train and the glittery hanging ornaments.

With Smokey for entertainment, our family snuggled together in the apartment while a glistening white cloak blanketed the outside world. Santa brought me a life-size Dance-With-Me doll with elastic straps on her feet. Her long blond pigtails mirrored my own shoulder-length curls. I also got a springy bouncing horse I called Dobbin. It was the happiest of holidays with my twin sister doll, Dobbin, and Smokey. There was no room to be only-child lonely. And I didn't yet know that there would be just a few cozy Christmases left in Rochester before Mother's holiday longings dictated that Christmas pilgrimages to Kansas City would become our requisite tradition.

Later that winter, I developed chicken pox right in the middle of the second-grade play preparations. Smokey was a loyal companion in my quarantine. But even that furry cuddler was unable to comfort me, the ailing Cinderella. I fretted. Would someone else be chosen for princess?

Providence intervened in the nick of time. Prince Charming too came down with chicken pox. He visited me, and amid bouts of itching, we practiced our parts to perfection. Other classmates got sick too. Our teacher rescheduled the play. Smokey purred. Mother applied the finishing touches, hundreds of tiny silver sequins, on my shimmering, white netted gown. The prince and I recovered, and the production debuted just after Valentine's Day. Smokey missed it, but he would soon star in a drama of his own.

Spring came to Rochester, as it must do. Smokey became a familiar prowler on the thawing grounds of Strathmore Circle. In those days, cats had both indoor and outdoor lives. More than once, I awoke to screeching nighttime howls below my window. My parents concocted an explanation of some sort. By then, our kitten had grown into adulthood, sporting a thick coat of regal gray fur, with no pedestrian patches of white, brown, or black. His mesmerizing green eyes shone even brighter than those which reflected from my adoring face.

We children conducted springtime forays throughout the blooming neighborhood, but Smokey grew lazier and fatter. No one seemed to notice when he began to remain indoors—too busy were we, cavorting in the fragrant spring air, absorbing precious rays of the brief summer sun.

There came a day when Smokey could be found neither inside nor out. Mother and I searched high and low. He was too fat to hide in his protected perch behind the kitchen stove. He was not in back of the couch—not under the bed—nor in the bedroom closets. Another closet in the hallway housed winter coats, mittens, scarves, blankets . . . various fleecy soft items enjoying a brief hibernation before the frosty days to come. It was in a dark corner of this cozy alcove that we discovered Smokey—nestling in a warm blanket, encircled by three dewy, mewling babies. "He" had become a mother.

"Kittens!" Kermit exploded.

Somehow, the little ones survived our clueless family long enough to go to forever homes (though not in trick-or-treat bags). Yet a conflict emerged in the Hill household. Mother could not abide the idea of a painful "procedure" for Smokey. I didn't know what that meant, but I was not in favor of anything that would hurt my precious pet.

A solution surfaced midway through Smokey's second pregnancy. Kermit, the rising young newspaper reporter and budding Man-About-Town, learned that a medical facility in Rochester was conducting research on blindness in newborn babies and needed litters of kittens for the study. Smokey became a donor mommy. She earned a shiny plaque—and a complimentary post-delivery "procedure"—assuring that no more mewling offspring would appear in the closets of 20 Strathmore Circle. Kermit wrote about Smokey in the *Rochester Democrat and Chronicle*. Her babies had contributed to a research breakthrough. Smokey achieved her fifteen minutes of fame, a scant year before her downfall.

Time moved on. The small Strathmore Circle apartment yielded to a three-bedroom bungalow just three miles away on Liberty Avenue. I traded little Abraham Lincoln School, built in 1926, for the brighter, bigger, newer halls of Durand-Eastman Elementary. Second grade became third, and then fourth—walking to school became bike riding. Kermit was now a recognized local newsman, and Violet cared for the house. Things bustled; I had many activities. Sometimes Smokey got lost in the shuffle. Hard to say where she spent her Christmases at this point, with our family bundling off to Kansas City each year. I wrote a story in class—a wish to remain in my cozy Rochester home with Mother, Father, and Smokey for Christmas, like times gone by.

While my father grew larger and busier in his growing career, it seemed that Mother began to shrink— wither—closing up like floral petals at dusk. Grandmother Zella visited us in Rochester—bringing a yellow "roller" canary, a hopeful ray of sunshine, in a cage. At her home in Kansas City, she raised these rare warblers with grim dedication—a singular bright spot in her own empty nest. Zella and dark moods were not strangers. She fretted over my mother and the canary, having little time or energy for me.

Smokey, with twitching tail, scrutinized the new arrival. The birdcage, mounted on a tall, sturdy stand, couldn't be cleaned unless the curious cat was secured elsewhere. Truth be told, I did not warm to the feathered creature, and my father would have nothing to do with it. We covered its cage with a cloth at night, so Father rarely saw it at all. Its cheerful warblings brought only fleeting smiles to Mother's wan face.

Now a busy schoolgirl, I thrived in our new child-rich, fun-filled neighborhood. Kermit worked at his newspapering; Grandmother Zella returned home. Mother—despite the canary's efforts—pined for her family in Kansas City.

In what turned out to be a harbinger of things to

come, Violet went into a hospital. I think there were rumors in the neighborhood, but no one told me what her problem was. Visits were not allowed. I helped tend the pets and escaped to my school-day routines. It was a long week: the house dusty, the animals and humans ragged. Much later, I wondered . . . could this have been the first of her dramatic cries for help?

And then—a homecoming. On unsteady legs, flanked by my father and me, Mother returned. Smokey rubbed and purred at her ankles . . . one last time. Our gazes shifted to the canary's post . . . now an awkward teetering cage, its door askew. An *empty* cage.

A trail of raggedy little yellow feathers led to my bedroom, and to a small, shocking pile—more feathers, some tiny, slickened bones. Smokey preened with pride until Kermit booted her down the basement steps. Mother took to her bed, sobbing. I helped to clean up the carnage and fretted about my beloved pet.

Never again did Smokey prowl that house or neighborhood. It was said that the celebrated cat had run away. There were no more cheerful chirpings—not much cheer at all in the Hill house. But over time, our muted routines resumed. And then, like a miracle worker, my father arrived home with an answer to our prayers . . . a tiny, wriggling black Cocker Spaniel puppy. Kermit, ever the newspaperman, named her Inky.

I had not a clue then, but Inky was the best of all that loomed ahead for my family on Liberty Avenue.

Beating the Clock

It is 1955. I am about eight years old. My father holds the handle of a long, straight-edged razor blade in each of his hands. He stands facing a volleyball net — feet apart, knees flexed, eyes riveted on my mother on the opposite side of the net. His muscles are as taut as violin strings,

Mother cradles a yellow balloon in her hands . . . a basket full of them in every color near her feet.

"Ready, set, go!"

She bats the balloon over the net. As it descends on the other side, my father advances forward. Clutching the razors, he traps the balloon and nudges it into a basket on the floor. It floats in on a tiny puff of air.

The audience roars. I leap up and down, clapping wildly and cheering from the sideline on stage. We are on "Beat the Clock," the television show, in New York City.

Mother lofts another balloon. My dad traps it between the

blades and guides it into the basket. The task is to transfer every balloon over the net without breaking a single one. My parents, an adroit team, do it — one by one — before the time runs out. They win!

The people picked my family, of all those seated in the audience, to come up on stage. Heartbeats pounded in my ears as Bud Collyer greeted and talked to my parents. I don't remember a thing he said, but soon the big clock started ticking and the game began. When it was over, Bud laughed and clapped and congratulated all of us. He even gave me a hug, though I had done nothing but cheer. He unveiled our prizes from behind heavy curtains: towels, sheets, and — the grand prize — an extensive power tool workshop. My father let out a loud whoop when he saw those tools and I spied a merry twinkle in my mother's eye, something rare.

A trip to New York City was an unusual happening for our family. Recreational travel was not the norm in those days. I never knew why it came about. Surely we did other things there, too. But my only recollection is "Beat the Clock." I wonder now if my father pulled some strings with one of his important friends to get us on the show. Maybe there was an ulterior motive . . . media exposure for him, the Rochester news reporter? Perhaps a change of scenery for my mother . . . to calm her jagged nerves? Later, I learned that there was a different clock ticking on that matter. A clock that would not be beaten so handily.

I wish I could remember more about that trip . . . my first-ever visit to "the Big Apple." The next time there, I would be thirteen years old and an outsider in my father's

28

retooled life.

My parents and I returned to Rochester to await our prizes, like the expectant family in *The Christmas Story*.

"At last!" we said, when the boxes came. They did not say "F-R-A-G-I-L-E," and they were not funny like the famous leg lamp with the fishnet stocking in the movie. But our prizes were bigger and just as exciting. We were all smiles, even Mother, as we tore into those promising packages.

"I am going to finish the basement," my father said, rubbing his hands together in anticipation. He set up a workshop and planned other rooms down there. We would hear his shiny tools whirring while scraps fell and our home filled with the clean smell of new lumber. Wood shavings flew like gentle snow on a wintry day, but my mother didn't complain about the dust.

"I like the smell of fresh wood," she said. I did too. And the little curly scraps reminded me of the springy blond curls of a favorite doll. Except for the splinters.

Thanks to my father's work and dedication, we ended up with a laundry area, the tool workshop, and a finished "rec" room—a room I later set up as the interior of an airplane to play Airline Stewardess, and in which other memorable events took place. Our house grew by fifty percent. The air felt lighter, warmer. As far as I could tell, my parents didn't talk about moving back to Kansas City. All because of an appearance on "Beat the Clock."

As the months of that year waned, however, the chills of fall crept inside on silent feet, like those of a stealthy kitten. Mother hugged herself tight. She cooked and cleaned, but her brow furrowed and her eyes grew dim. When she looked that way, my stomach tied itself into a knot. My father was away a lot, and when he was home, he had less to say. I missed his smiles and his silly jokes. Sometimes my parents had hushed discussions—I overheard whispers about "Kansas City." Finally, I learned things were about to change. The novelty of some bright linens, fresh wood scents and a new basement had worn off.

In December, I wrote to Bud Collyer. My letter, eight-year-old style, would have gone like this:

Dear Mr. Collyer,

My family was on "Beat the Clock." My dad caught all the balloons with razor blades and won some tools. He made us a new basement. But now my mother doesn't want to live here anymore. She wants to move to Kansas City. My dad is trying to find a job there. I only want one thing for Christmas so I am writing to you, not Santa Claus. Can you help my dad find a job? He is a good newspaper reporter. Thank you.
--Nancy Hill

I never got an answer to that letter, and my father did not get a job in Kansas City. Turns out, that's not what he wanted after all.

Reading Comprehension

*L*ike a broken record, I repeated the mantra to my chagrined parents. "I really, really want a baby brother or sister. My friends are always getting them. Please, please get me one." I was an only child who pined for a sibling. I took every opportunity to let my parents know this.

They looked at the floor and said, as always, "It doesn't happen quite like that."

"Well, however it happens, I really want one."

My parents gave me books, they gave me my beloved Inky dog—but no siblings.

One evening, Mother brought out a book. It wasn't like the books I owned or borrowed from the library. There was a picture of a girl and her mother on the cover, not very interesting. It was flimsy and didn't have a lot of pages. The best books had lots of pages.

"This is for you to read."

Mother said the book would explain how babies were gotten. She handed it to me. I barely listened as she said, "I want you to talk to me if you have questions."

I opened the book in bed that night. It had strange pictures and drawings. The story was unlike any I had ever heard. I had trouble falling asleep.

The next morning was Saturday, and I got up before my parents. Puzzling over the odd little book while eating dry cereal outside on our breezeway, I looked up to see my friend Angie. Angie and I were in the same third-grade class and she lived right across the street. Without thinking, I said to her, "Look at this."

We pored over every part of that precise little book, scrunching up our faces. Angie had brothers, so she understood the pictures better than I did. As we paged and paged through the strange book, my mother came out on the breezeway.

"What are you doing?" she asked. Her voice sounded loud and her face was red. Our own voices stuck in our throats.

"Just looking at the book you gave me to read," I said, with hooded eyes.

Mother sent Angie home and called her mother right away. They talked for a long time. I had to wait in my room. Mother may have informed my father, too. I think he spent most of that day in his workshop with his power tools. He did not talk to me about the book.

"Why did you show that book to Angie?" Mother asked.

"You didn't tell me not to. We share all our books."

My gaze did not rise to meet my mother's.

"But this book is private. If you had questions, I wanted you to talk to me."

What could I say? It made my stomach hurt to think about asking questions about that book.

"I didn't have questions."

I don't remember what we said after that, or what happened to that curious little book, but I know I didn't ask for a brother or sister again. And there wasn't one, until later . . . in another life.

Book Worm

*H*aving resigned myself to the idea that I would always be an only child, I took refuge in books. They kept me company on lonely days and helped me to fall asleep at night. I treasured them as if they were a stash of gold on the shelves in my room. During the school year, I couldn't wait for library day. One summer, Angie and I discovered the local public library.

We talked our parents into letting us ride our bikes to the library — a major accomplishment, since we had to walk them across a wide, busy road to get there. Of course, we never admitted to being scared. Could it be that our mothers were glad to have us out from underfoot?

Once we reached the library — out of breath and sweaty — the cool and calm would wash over us like a gentle wave. We sensed its unique, dusky smell — a smell of peace and quiet. Unlike the uneasy quiet which sometimes filled my home.

"Ah . . . here are my friends!" the smiling librarian would say.

One afternoon, the librarian asked if we would like to help her shelve the returned books. She taught us the rudiments of the Dewey decimal system, just enough to do the job. We liked it so much we went twice a week to help her that summer. The work was a lot more interesting than the minor jobs I had at home. And the library always felt organized, calm and secure.

The librarian called us "trusty volunteers." We beamed. And our reward was choosing and loading up cargo as we finished . . . precious new books to read, which the librarian helped us select. I pumped hard on the pedals of my bike in anticipation of cracking the covers of that treasured bounty. To escape to new worlds within those pages.

The seed of an idea came from my job. It brought a smile to my mother's face.

"I am going to make my own library in our basement."

I gathered all my Little Golden Books together. They made a tall stack—those beloved books I had outgrown. Mother got the supplies I needed. I cut oak-tag pockets, glued them in the front of each Golden Book, made a card to insert in each pocket, and with a ruler lined the cards in small sections like the ones at the library. This took weeks. I did the work in our new basement "wreck" room. With its funny name for a room kept so neat and tidy, the room smelled of newly sawn wood and fresh linoleum glue . . . not like the library, but nice. I made up some sort of numbering system with random decimal points, giving each book a number and placing it in order on our new bookshelves. Everything felt organized and peaceful. After I added a few folding chairs and a card table, my library was ready.

There were a lot of children in our neighborhood, many of them younger than me. "Come to see my new library," I said, and they did.

The organization turned to chaos. The little ones didn't follow my directions at all. Only a few of them could write their names on the little cards. They just wanted to take all the books down and pretend to read them, and they made a lot of noise.

"You have to be quiet in a library!"

My hissed pleadings had no effect.

Even with Angie's help, I couldn't make it work like an actual library. It wasn't long before the kids tired of the activity. When they went home, I breathed a huge sigh. It was a lot of work to collect all the books and arrange them back on the shelves . . . to restore order and peace to my little oasis of books.

My parents chuckled at me and my basement library; Mother showed it to her friends. She would lead them downstairs and, with pride in her eyes, say, "Look what Nancy has done with her Golden Books."

Though my love of books lived on, it turned out that my little library did not stand the test of time. It was still there when we moved away. The little books remained on the shelves, lonely and dusty and leaning askew, as if pointing the way to the ragged times soon to come.

Little Bear's Den

One typical winter day in Rochester, complete with a deep blanket of snow outside and icicles dangling over our porch, I wandered about the house. My father called down the hall.

"Nancy . . . " I stopped in my tracks. But he hadn't said 'Nancy Ann.' So it didn't sound like I was in trouble. "Why don't we do some work in the den?"

Beneath my smile, I breathed a silent 'whew.'

I headed into that cozy wood-clad room with the large oak desk and rolling, swiveling chair — his office when he was at home. The room my mother never entered, but into which he sometimes invited me. The room in which I, with my writer father, sensed — for the first time — the magic of writing.

"Let's see what Little Brown Bear is doing today," Dad said. He opened the closet door and extracted a few of the immense pieces of blank newsprint he always brought home from work. The creamy white paper with tiny brown flecks reflected the golden glow of the den's warm knotty-pine paneling. The empty expanses of those pages begged to be filled; together we had inscribed many of them with the mischievous adventures of a little brown bear. Sitting next to each other on the nubby green couch across from his desk, we had concocted vivid sentences and paragraphs of fascinating bear activities.

"What can Little Bear be up to on this snowy day?" Dad asked — to get us going.

"He should have a scary adventure," I said.

My father recorded our thoughts with a marker on that creamy paper, but not until each string of words was correct, logical, grammatical. When I suggested a thought, he said, "Let's think. Does that make sense here?"

Over weeks and months, our story had grown longer, more dramatic, more fun. Little Bear got into and out of trouble. He made friends and enemies in the forest. But things would always turn out okay for him, at least for a while.

Sometimes my father and I would get crayons or water paints and create illustrations to go along with the stories. He liked that—I wasn't so good at it. I much preferred to dream up the adventures for our little friend. But the pictures made the sentences more real. That bear 'book' grew thicker and thicker. Together we would read through the whole thing before starting on a new story.

"Each of our stories is a chapter," Dad said, as we finished the bear's antics for the day.

I grinned. "Just like the chapters in my library books."

He rolled the huge pages up and tied the precious bundle together to tuck away in the closet. In Little Bear's Den, with the other pieces we had written. "All safe, until next time," he said.

I remember a sad. somber time in the den, one that was not about our young bear friend. I spent most of that evening crying on the couch. In the afternoon, a sliding car had struck our beloved Inky dog on the icy street right in front of our house. I had held her, shivering in a thick blanket, as we drove to the vet. Her raspy breaths knifed into my heart. The kind old man who doctored her told us she had dislocated her hip.

"I can fix Inky up," he said in a soft voice, "but you will have to let her spend the night here with me." We left her with that gentle man and I sobbed all the way home. My mother sniffled and my dad drove with jaw clenched and steely eyes fixed on the road ahead. Frozen white flakes swirled around us as we inched along, as if encased within a sad little snow globe.

For once, my father said I didn't have to eat dinner. Instead, he made a big bowl of cheese popcorn and let me take it to curl up on the nubby green couch with a favorite book. It was about another Cocker Spaniel. As I ate the buttery yellow bits of cheesy corn, heart aching, I came upon a piece that reminded me of Inky. Though gold, not black, it seemed to have a sweet little face and long floppy ears. With tender care, I placed the special golden puff into a clean ashtray on the end table. It looked back and calmed me as I read in the warm light of the tawny den, as though Inky lay alongside watching over me.

After a while, my father came in. "How are you doing?" he asked. I knew we would not work on our bear stories that night. He sat and swiveled in his rolling chair across from the couch.

He bent his head and leaned over close to me, whispering, "I think Inky is going to be okay." Comforted by his muted, hopeful tones, I stopped crying. We shared some popcorn.

It happened in an instant. My dad reached to the ashtray.

"And what is this?" he asked in a playful tone. Ever the jokester, he quipped, "A piece of popcorn got out and ran away." With that, he popped the stray bit into his mouth and swallowed it right down. I gasped. My eyes filled with tears once again. My voice froze in my throat. How could I explain about saving that piece because it reminded me of Inky? I knew my dad didn't like crying, but I couldn't stop. He rose and said in a gruff tone, "It's time for bed."

I followed my father out of the golden glow of the den and padded down the hall to my room—alone—to tunnel under the chilly covers like a moth encased in a lonely cocoon. He did not come to tuck me in, but Mother did, and we shared a tearful hug.

Inky came back home with her hip intact. We were cautious and protective of her for months. Once, on an icy patch, that hip popped out again. But, as things turned out, that sweet pup weathered her own injuries and, within a year, those that dislocated our family far more seriously than Inky's hip— or the loss of a tiny kernel of cheese-coated comfort on a sad snowy evening in a golden paneled den. And a next time that would never come for a Little Brown Bear.

How to Learn that Winning Isn't Everything

Winning isn't everything. This is a lesson to be learned early in life. For me, at about age nine. It is good if you live in a neighborhood with prolific families . . . moms, dads, lots of kids. Especially if you are an only child.

My neighborhood in Rochester was East Irondequoit. Liberty Avenue. There was one other Catholic family on our block, and they had children of every age and size. Even the Protestant family across the street had three children. The neighbors became my siblings. We all rode bikes, ice-skated and trick-or-treated, but the competitive activity of choice was pogo-stick jumping. Pogo competition depended upon a lot of factors.

1. *Everyone should have a pogo stick like everyone else's.*

In those days, pogo sticks came in only one basic

model. We all had one. Mine was red, and I loved it.

2.   *Someone needs to have a long, wide, level driveway.*

I lived in the middle of the block on the lower side of the street. My driveway was perfect . . . the center of our universe when it came to pogo contests.

3.   *The parents who live in the house with the perfect driveway must either not know or not care that sometimes the rubber foot on the bottom of the pogo stick gets worn. In that case, the hollow metal end of the stick clangs into the driveway with every jump, leaving small circular indentations – cuts – in the asphalt.*

My mother knew but pretended she didn't. My father didn't know.

4.   *Participants must be available right after dinner each evening in the summer for what could be hours. No saying, "I just ate." No calling home or leaving early because of a curfew.*

The parents on my block were quite happy to send their kids out of the house right after dinner. In those times, cocktails were consumed both before *and* after dinner, although I didn't realize that until later.

5.   *One of the kids must be in charge of getting everyone all lined up and ready and going over the rules – like: no bumping into anyone and, if even <u>one</u> foot comes off the stick and touches the ground, you're out.*

At my house and in my driveway, the one in charge was usually me.

6.   *Everyone has to count their jumps out loud in a coordinated cadence. Uniform jumping speed must be observed.*

That was easy. There really is only one successful speed on a pogo stick.

Not too slow — you'll fall off. Not too fast — you'll fall off.

Learning that winning isn't everything is counterintuitive to young kids. To them, winning IS everything. Maybe not the ONLY thing, but nearly. Sometimes it takes a wakeup call for this important lesson to sink in. And sometimes that wakeup call comes in the form of a legendary pogo match.

*   *   *

We "regulars" convened in the driveway after dinner, racing to the end where the asphalt was hardest. We didn't have Daylight Savings Time back then, but it was still light out. No need to go over the rules with this group of veteran jumpers . . . Angie, her brothers, and me. Our pogo sticks whipped into place and we assumed the starting position.

"Ready, set, go." We were off.

It took a moment or two to get going, but we achieved our rhythm quickly. "Okay. Time to count!"

One . . . two . . . three . . . four . . . The trick was to stay in the same spot and jump as long as you could. Our counting was loud enough; no one could cheat. At seventy hops, I had only one opponent left, one of Angie's brothers. The others formed a ring around us, chanting. At eighty-three, he clattered to the ground. I was the victor!

"Okay. You won. Come on, get down. You know we always do two out of three."

"No!" I was now at ninety-five, no longer gasping

for breath. "Start again if you want. I'm going on."

I had achieved that state of perfect balance and rhythm that might have enabled me to jump forever. My counting became unconscious. Perhaps, as I looked around the neighborhood in my autonomic bouncing state, I thought of our fun but frosty Halloweens and Easters. Or did I stare at that hateful spot on Liberty Avenue where my beloved Cocker Spaniel, Inky, was once struck by a skidding car? Maybe I could see as far as the grassy meadow way down the street, where Angie and I used to spend lazy summer days labeling puffy clouds or searching in vain for four-leaf clovers (that is, until the afternoon when our private musings were interrupted by a weird stranger in an unseemly trench coat, which he ceremoniously opened before our virginal eyes).

Who knows what was going through my happy, hopping mind? I was setting the All-Time Record! Me, of all people!

The others kicked the blacktop, rolled their eyes. Even Angie.

"Come on, Nancy. That's enough!"

"I'm not quitting!"

"No fair!" They headed off, grumbling. Their pogo sticks scraped and clattered.

I didn't care. My personal victory was all that mattered. Somewhere around two hundred, I grew tired and hopped off. In the sun's waning summer rays, my shadow looked like I was six feet tall.

As though on wings, I flew inside the house to tell Mom and Dad. Red faced, I raced through the kitchen holding my breath. When I entered the dining room, I came up short. Dinner had been over for at least an hour, but the crusty dishes sat untouched on the table. I saw half-empty highball glasses and sad, shrinking ice cubes. The sweat on my brow chilled as if I had been flash frozen. Two furrowed faces jerked up to look at me. I noted brimming eyes. An unlikely question flashed through my head: *Will I get to tell them my news?*

A heartbeat's pause. My mother's voice quavered. "Honey, your father and I have something to tell you." Somehow, I knew the next words were going to change everything.

I probably started to cry even before Mother muttered that she and my father had decided it would be best not to live together or be married anymore.

The frozen scene — mother, father, messy table — swam before me. Someone said a word I barely knew. A word that was alien in my little 1950s suburban Catholic world ... DIVORCE. The word that, indeed, changed everything.

It took only two syllables to eclipse the news I had raced in to share.

Victory lost.

Lesson learned.

Winning isn't everything, after all.

(The following is adapted from the well-loved children's song released by Swingset Mamas, "Mamamorphosis," 2011)

Oh little playmate
Come out and play with me
And bring your dollies three
Climb up my apple tree
Look down my rain barrel
Slide down my cellar door
And we'll be jolly friends
Forever more.

So sorry playmate
I cannot play with you
My dolly's got the flu
Boo hoo hoo hoo hoo hoo
Ain't got no rain barrel
Ain't got no cellar door
Won't have my jolly friends
Forever more.

There Once Was A Dad

We are in the bathroom. In our house on Liberty Avenue. I am sitting on the edge of the bathtub — the same edge over which he sometimes makes me bend to receive the brandishments of a hairbrush. He wears blue boxer shorts with a towel draping his damp shoulders. Fluffy puffs of cream adorn his cheeks and craggy chin. Ordinarily I would think of Santa Claus, but not this day. The fogged mirror reflects a toweled-off swipe in the middle. Within that cleared space is a serious face and deep brown craters of eyes.

The man with his back to me is my dad, my hero. As he shaves with more deliberation than is usual, my gaze drifts to the hazy window and my ten-year-old head overflows with his aspect.

-----*He works hard as a newspaperman. He has a nice office, and a lot of people know who he is.*

-----*He likes to write for, and with, me — on big sheets of newsprint he brings home from work. How I love those clean sheets, just itching to be filled with our words and pictures.*

-----*He can be funny. He makes me laugh. Silly voices. Jokes. Goofy faces.*

-----*He builds things for me, like my cherished swing set behind the house and the unique little ice-skating rink on the upper terrace of our yard. He even built a rec room in our basement.*

-----*He can make me cry . . . when I have to bend over the bathtub for a spanking or sit on a stool in the kitchen corner facing the wall for an hour, like the time I left Lick-M-Aid wrappers under the swing set. I cry not because he hurts me, but because I have disappointed him.*

-----*Once he made a valiant attempt to teach me to swim in the near freezing, rocky-bottomed Lake Canandaigua. I shivered, shook, and cried. Turns out he was a former WWII frogman, but I didn't know that then — nor that his genes would later launch in me a lifelong passion for swimming, a devotion to water.*

-----*He knows a lot of important people, like the people who invited me to be a model on TV for a local Rochester Easter special, even though I was too chubby to fit properly into any of the fashions that the other girls — those little blonde waifs — were wearing. I can still see the red, black and white dress they finally found for me to wear, and I can almost feel it cutting into my waist where the zipper was extended precariously with pins. My dress, unlike theirs, did not look Eastery at all — and, among the other sparkling faces, my forced smile reflected only pain. I was not invited again.*

-----*He can cry, too. In tears, he prayed on his knees in a candlelit pew of Annunciation Church in Rochester the evening he* learned his father, not yet sixty, had died of a heart attack. I cried and prayed also; I liked Grandfather Hill. Since my mother and I didn't go to Kansas City for the funeral, I never got to say goodbye to my grandfather.

-----He gave me a little Kodak Brownie camera to cherish. He likes to take pictures and taught me to take them too. Taking pictures is fun; we have quite a collection of them. I have wondered why there are no pictures of my mother when she was pregnant with me. I once asked my parents if I was adopted, but they laughed and said no.

-----He likes to take me ice-skating when the magical Rochester winters arrive. I tried to become a good skater so he would be proud of me, but when I broke my arm on a neighborhood pond in fourth grade, my ice-skating lessons at the Rochester Institute of Technology ended. I still hope to make my father proud of me as a skater.

-----He says he loves me more than anything in the world.

My dad snaps the towel from his shoulders and dries his unsmiling face, ending my reverie. My heart lurches; my lip quivers. I stare at his image in the mirror, trying to memorize that handsome face. He is almost ready to go — to work, to somewhere.

"You know that leaving you is going to be the hardest thing I will ever do in my life, don't you?"

My head drops; my heart stops. A hug. And then he is gone.

Thirteen

*O*n what seemed like an instant, my dad had become my "father." A father reviled by my mother. I didn't see him again for three years.

That father invited me to Rochester . . . much to my mother's dismay. She cried when she took me to the airport. Though my mouth was bone dry, I pasted a small smile to my lips.

I loved flying in airplanes when seated between my parents — but going all by myself was another matter. It didn't help that it was Friday, the 13th, and I was 13 years old.

Kermit greeted me in New York with a huge grin and a bear hug. In his embrace, I felt as if I might disappear like a puff of smoke. His characteristic booming voice vibrated my eardrums.

"It is just great to see you! We're going to have a

wonderful time."

Again, I pasted on a smile even as my legs quivered. He kept up a round of questions and banter as we drove toward what I knew were his new wife and her two children, now adopted by my father. I twisted my hair and turned my head to chew on a fingernail.

Their house, in Pittsford, was long and sleek ... smoky glass and angles. A house whose severe countenance looked wrong to me. I did not grow up to become a fan of contemporary architecture.

On the back terrace, around the swimming pool, I met Betty and her children. The bleached streak in Betty's coal black hair was brighter than her simulated smile and hot-pink lipstick. I banished a fleeting vision of a skunk. Her heavy gold jewelry clinked and flashed in the bright sunlight. The daughter, two years my junior, squirmed at her mother's side and scuffed her sandals on the pool deck. A shaky smile peeked from below the girl's hooded eyes. Her younger brother shot a grin at me before racing back into the water. I bit my lip.

Kermit beamed as he watched his stepchildren swim and dive like fish, calling them "little minnows." Did he recall — as did I, with a painful pang — a tortuous afternoon years ago at nearby Lake Canandaigua . . . one on which he had attempted without success to teach me to swim?

Tanned, spunky, wiry — those stepchildren were precious. At thirteen, I was neither wiry nor precious. Pale-skinned, poolside and wishing for the shell of a turtle, I counted the hours until bedtime.

My father showed me the guest room and left me to

prepare for bed. I crawled beneath the covers, trying to warm my frosty toes and frozen heart. I was sniffling when he came to say goodnight. He hated crying, how well I remembered — but there was nothing I could do to stem the tears.

"What's the matter, Nancy? Aren't you happy to be here?"

Happy? How could I describe the reeling in my head? My wounded mind grappled with the contrasts of this opulent existence with the tense, spare life Mother and I maintained in Kansas City. Betty's striped coiffure . . . my mother's soft chestnut tresses. Her sparkling fingers and golden wrists . . . Mother's own fingers, as unembellished as her checkbook balance. The spirited sibling camaraderie . . . my listless and lonely solo situation.

"Just a little homesick, I guess," I said, around the edges of a teary smile.

"Well, that won't last long. We are going to have a great time. Sleep tight." He patted me on the head as he turned and left the room. He didn't mention that we would visit Betty's wealthy parents in the imposing contemporary house next door. At least there I would lose myself in front of the massive aquarium wall bubbling with exotic plants and flamboyant fishes.

I cried myself to sleep. My toes and heart were still cold in the morning. At the vulnerable age of thirteen, I had realized that being in that place with that family was lonelier than being without a father.

When the visit ended, I encased my feelings in a numb cocoon. I went back to Mother and our little one-bedroom apartment and didn't see my father again for sixteen years.

We Meet Again

$\mathcal{I}$ was almost thirty — wife, mother, teacher — when the telephone trilled. The year was 1976. The sixteen-year-old cocoon in my heart was in place, intact.

"Nancy, this is your father." Although we had exchanged birthday cards and the occasional letter over the years, a phone call was rare. My breath stuck in my throat.

"Well, hello."

We shared some brief pleasantries before he said, "I have good news. I am coming to the Republican National Convention next month. I'd like to get together with you." A fault line in my heart shifted slightly. Despite a creased brow, my pulse quickened.

I knew the convention was to be held in Kansas City, where John and I had settled after college ... Kermit's hometown and ours.

"Well, yes. Wow. That'll be great." My hand quivered

on the receiver. I fiddled with the curly phone cord.

"I'm hoping you can take me on a tour of my old houses, my schools and my haunts in the city," he said. "And, of course, to your home to meet John and my grandson."

And that's what happened. My father came to the 1976 convention and inserted himself into my grown-up life.

We drove about town to see the places where he had lived. The highlight of the day was his beloved Paseo High School. At our house in Raytown, he met John and our young son, his first and only grandson. I wore a lime green, polyester pantsuit with a bright flowered scarf around my frosted blond bob. We did not discuss the fact that I had not invited him to my wedding.

Kermit secured passes for John and me to attend the convention. At the time, my father was the head of public relations for the New York Republican Party.

At the convention on Day One, I waited for Kermit in the back corner of a chilly conference room in the Kemper Arena, wishing I had brought a sweater to cover my sleeveless voile A-line dress with the white pearl buttons — the same emerald green dress I had worn to my bridal luncheon eight years prior. The dress summoned the memory of how I had caved to my mother's tearful stance against inviting Kermit to my wedding.

An entourage of brash press folks swooped in with their microphones thrust in the face of an imposing bald fellow. The man, chair of the NY party and delegation, was there for a press conference. He took to the podium and bellowed, "Where's Kermit? I don't say a word without

Kermit!"

I curled myself tighter together in the corner and held my breath until Kermit arrived and spoke. I had to clench my hands together to keep from biting my fingernails.

When he rescued me, my father introduced me to a dignitary or two and we spent a few moments together before he rushed off to another meeting. I didn't see him again, but John and I will always remember our time at that tumultuous convention, where Gerald Ford survived a raucous challenge from Ronald Reagan to become the Republican presidential nominee. Though Ford then failed in his quest to beat Jimmy Carter for president, I succeeded in establishing a renewed — if tentative — connection with my father.

Kermit began inviting us to New York to spend annual Thanksgivings with him and his family — the family which never attained "stepfamily" status in my scarred heart. Betty would always be "my father's wife," never my "stepmother." We got along and, over the years, forged a fragile friendship. To her, I was "Kermit's daughter." Once she told me that she was not responsible for my parents' divorce . . . that she wasn't "the other woman."

The two of them had moved to rural Albany, and those were Currier and Ives holidays — complete with blankets of deep snow, roaring fires, and bottomless servings of my father's famous Bloody Marys.

"The only way to make a Bloody Mary," he would say, "is with Clamato juice and lots of fresh horseradish." There were other undisclosed ingredients. To this day, if a Bloody Mary doesn't cause my glands to twinge, it's not worth the calories.

During those adult visits, I learned what a distinguished Navy man Kermit had been—a frogman of UDT 21, defusing mines in Tokyo Harbor and completing other harrowing missions. I had a hard time wrapping my head around such skill, such courage. He and John discussed the details; I sat with mouth agape and listened.

Kermit spoke of his heady position as a young press correspondent at the White House before my birth and during our early years in D.C.

"My knees would knock as I flashed my credentials," he said. "I couldn't believe I worked at the White House. I always expected someone to throw me out on my ear." He had been twenty-four years old.

We saw pictures of Kermit with Truman, Eisenhower, Rockefeller, other dignitaries. He spoke of the ambitious public relations firm he and Betty had founded in Rochester, and how they became a local power-couple about the city. With clenched jaw, I viewed their pictures in the society column pages.

"We took a big risk, starting that firm," he said. "You've got to be willing to take risks to get what you want in life."

I thought about risk. I knew there was risk in divorce, of course. In remarriage, even to a woman with wealthy parents living right next door. And there was some risk in adopting her two young children, financing their educations, and securing them jobs and careers, one with the Professional Golf Association. Clearly, my father did not shy away from risk—including the risk involved in leaving and then failing to support his only biological child.

I sighed at the irony. How my own college education was paid for not just by my single-mother's blood, sweat and tears — but also by my own success in earning scholarships, grants, loans, and summer jobs. And how, with fierce determination, I had sought, applied for, and gotten every one of my career positions all by myself.

My father isn't the only risk taker in the family, I mused.

Father Is as Father Does

The year Kermit turned sixty, I learned what a father isn't. By then, I was in my mid-thirties with a husband, two growing sons, a satisfying career of my own, and a Hansel-and-Gretel, ivy clad stone cottage of a home in suburban Pittsburgh. Those blessings softened the blow.

That year we were not invited to New York for Thanksgiving.

"We can't have Thanksgiving together this year," Kermit called to say. "Betty and I are not speaking to each other."

"Okay...."

"Yeah. She made a promise that she would quit smoking for a year. I told her I'd pay her $500 for that, and I did."

"It's good she quit smoking," I said, sure that this was not the end of the story.

"Not so fast. I found out that she didn't quit after all. Turns out, she's been going out to the barn and smoking on the sly."

I could just picture Betty, bundled in fur against the chill winds of Albany, sneaking out to puff away in one of the horse's stalls, diamond earrings ablaze.

"So I told her I'm not going to speak to her for a year." I was sure he nodded his head with conviction.

That year was not yet over. Same house, same day-to-day life, no communication. For 365 days. My father was a man of his word. And that white streak in Betty's hair spelled s-t-u-b-b-o-r-n with a capital S.

"Well, why don't you come here to have Thanksgiving with us instead?" I asked into the receiver, shielding a growing grin. My heart quickened in anticipation.

Despite our happy preparations, I remember only one episode from that unique Thanksgiving holiday. Kermit, as he was about to depart, asked to speak to me in private.

"You need to know that no male in my family has ever lived beyond sixty years of age, and I am due to turn sixty in May," he said.

He proceeded to unpack papers and to fill me in on the details of his end-of-life plan. It was simple—his estate would be split three ways: one-third to each of his stepchildren, and one-third to his wife for living expenses until she died. His only biological child—that would be me—would receive what was left of Betty's portion of the estate upon her death.

Dazed, I said nothing. Like a punch to the stomach, his words had taken my voice away. While the monetary impact meant little, the realization that he had omitted me — his only child — as a primary family member caused my head to spin. I muttered a weary assent.

"I see."

I told him I understood the details in the folder he presented to me. The words cut like icicles into my tongue.

Kermit packed up his papers with brisk efficiency and prepared to leave. He glanced at his calendar.

"Oh, good. When I get home, the year will be over. Betty and I will be speaking to each other again."

"Don't count on it," I said.

I was right. That is, until his heart attack in the spring. Just before his sixtieth birthday in May, Betty called.

"Your father has had a heart attack. We are helicoptering him to Cleveland Clinic. I will keep you posted."

"Thank you, Betty." A warm tear rolled down my cheek.

And later, "He's going to be all right."

"That's a relief," I said. "And now you two can start speaking to each other again."

"Don't count on it," she said.

His Closing Chapter

*K*ermit Hill lived until he was eighty. During those extra twenty years, he moved to Pinehurst, North Carolina, where he took photos, played golf every day until he couldn't . . . and wrote. Once he called to ask if I would read and react to the draft of a book he had composed—a Greatest-Generation-type story about his life. I agreed. It was long and not particularly well-written, yet compelling to me. I scoured every page, anxious to find myself, and my mother. We did not appear as characters in any chapter. I found us in the *POSTSCRIPT*:

"On a personal note, in November 1944, very shortly before the author was ordered overseas in World War II, he and his high school and college 'steady' were married in West Palm Beach, Florida. As with so many wartime marriages that were followed by long wartime separations and the strains and tensions of postwar resettlement, the marriage did not work out despite several efforts

at reconciliation. The marriage produced a daughter, who graduated from the University of Missouri and has a successful career in education. Her mother is deceased."

I called to offer my feedback. "The book is informative, eye-opening. I learned a lot."

I refrained from sharing a critique of his writing skills or commenting about my absence in the narrative—which curiously paralleled my meager presence in his will. In 2003, he self-published *Those Were the Days . . . the 1900s . . . a Century of Drama*. My copy collected dust until I embarked upon my own memoir fifteen years later.

In the two decades following Kermit's heart attack, our visits were less frequent. I had taken up golf, but my skills never approached his once single-digit handicap. In fact, in all my life, we shared only nine holes of golf—during a Thanksgiving visit to Pinehurst. Like the lower handicapper he was, he played well. I did not. He didn't appear to notice. I figured that since his adopted children were excellent golfers—having grown up with him as their mentor, playing on country club teams—my marginal performance was of little consequence. Still, I disappointed myself in that one chance to show him my abilities.

Nearing age eighty, my father stopped eating.

"Why?" I asked.

"I've lived a great life, published two books, done everything I want to do. I'm finished."

With only a daily cocktail as sustenance, he proceeded to starve himself. He would not let our sons, adults by then, make a final visit, but he agreed that my husband and I could come.

To prepare for the harrowing trip, I assembled a booklet for my father. Called "Pieces of the Writer's Daughter," it was a collection of twenty-five years of writings of my own ... professional, personal, serious, whimsical. I laminated a colorful, rudimentary binding and penned an inscription:

To my Father on the Occasion of his 80th Birthday

... a father who, with the help of a little brown bear, showed me the path to a lifelong love of writing

... a father who showed me that it is never too late to publish a first book

... a father whose gift for writing lives on in his daughter and both of his grandsons

With love and gratitude for a legacy of fortitude, achievement, leadership, and of the courage it takes to live one's life as a dream-seeker ... Nancy   May 10, 2004

The booklet traveled to Pinehurst in my suitcase. Our visit was tense and short. We were allowed what seemed like only moments to sit beside his skeleton-like, bedridden frame. I told him of my lifelong love of writing, thanked him and presented the booklet. He glanced at the cover.

"You can take that back home with you," he said. My reddened cheeks throbbed as I left it there, unopened upon his bedcovers.

The last words I heard my father say were, "I've had a great life ... and a great wife." He smiled vacantly at her, not at me. I left his side for the final time, feeling as though a wrecking ball had careened into the center of my heart. Weak as he was, my father still retained the power to demolish.

The booklet I had prepared for him came back to me in the mail after his death—together with military medals, scrapbooks, other artifacts of his life, and a short, cryptic note from Betty. She lived on for many years, but our fragile relationship lasted only a few months beyond my father's final breath.

That father of mine, Kermit Eugene Hill, was a tough-minded product of tough years and times ... a self-promoter, a doer, an achiever. And a tough man to have had as a parent.

In my time I have known great fathers—people like my husband, my son, and the man who became my stepfather. Kermit Hill brought me to life—maybe to golf and swimming, no doubt to writing—probably to my dogged determination to persevere, to achieve. It is not for his fathering but for those things that I thank him. And, of course, for that matchless Bloody Mary recipe.

The Secret

One spring, people on Liberty Avenue awoke to a surprise—a FOR SALE sign in front of the house across the street from ours. A lot of cars came and left, left and came. Dressed-up people with clipboards and briefcases and serious faces went in and out. Neighbors scratched their heads, whispering over back fences. The people who were moving didn't have children, so I didn't pay much attention. I did hope some new children would move in, though.

On our street, in Rochester, New York, in the mid-1950s, people knew what was happening with one another. Children of all ages played together. There were sleepovers for the kids, cookouts, adult cocktail hours and bridge groups. The yards sported bikes, pogo sticks, swing sets, and even a small but popular ice-skating rink that my father built on our terrace. The generous families shared many things . . . babysitters, ladders, lawnmowers, cups of sugar, information. Later, I learned about something else they shared on Liberty Avenue. A secret.

After that house went up for sale, something unusual began in our basement. Meetings of the neighbors. To this, I did pay attention.

"We don't want you to talk about the meetings," my parents said. It was an odd thing for them to say.

Though curious, I did not ask or talk about the gatherings that took place downstairs. People frowned or looked at their shoes while coming and going; it was clear they weren't having cocktails or playing bridge. Most of the meetings were quiet, even hushed, but sometimes voices grew loud enough to carry into my room upstairs. The words were not clear, but the tones gave me goosebumps. Still, I didn't ask.

After a time, a SOLD sign went up across the street. A new family moved in. They seemed young—a father, a mother, a new baby. They looked just like every other family on the block; however, they kept to themselves. When Mother and I took an Easter basket over, they didn't answer the door, so we left it on the porch. I really wanted to play with their baby, but I never got to do that, since a few months after the family moved in, my Liberty Avenue world collapsed. Mother and I left to live with my grandparents in Kansas City. As if torn from a womb.

After the bitter divorce, Mother was angry with my father. She voiced frequent complaints. I would cringe, but she continued to grumble on.

"Nancy, I want you to know something your father did," Mother said one day. "Do you remember all those meetings he held in our basement when the house across the street was for sale?" I remembered.

"You should know what those meetings were all about. It was the dark secret of Liberty Avenue." When that house went up for sale, Mother said, some real estate "speculators" wanted it. "When your father got wind of this, he got all the neighbors together. He did not want that to happen and neither did most of the neighbors."

"Why not?" I asked, and wished I hadn't.

Most of Mother's explanation was incomprehensible to me, revolving around real estate terminology and other adult concepts. I tuned her out, wishing to be somewhere else. But she went on.

"Here's what happened. Your father and the neighbors figured out how to prevent the speculators from getting the house. Somehow, they found a family that wanted to buy it but didn't have enough money. The neighbors and your father took up a collection and gave the money to that family so they had enough to buy the house. Everything was a big secret."

I wondered if this was the reason that new family kept to themselves, since they really didn't buy their house on their own. Maybe they were embarrassed to have taken money from the neighbors. Or were the others unhappy to have given it? This disconnect was unusual in our friendly area. For reasons I couldn't explain, this story gave me a bad feeling.

According to my mother, organizing those meetings was bad . . . one more bad thing my father had done. The idea was confusing to me as a ten-year-old. At that stage, I had thought it was nice of the neighbors to help a young family and I wished I could stop the litanies of complaints from my mother.

The secret of Liberty Avenue percolated in my head for years. Much later, I found out that similar proceedings had gone on in other places, too, and I learned the sorry underpinnings of such practices. My innocent introduction to social injustice, indeed prejudice, had come on the heels of the deeply troubling times which had begun to unfold and spread across the country. I felt sorrow — and shame — for my father, the neighbors, and the unwitting witnesses such as myself.

Still, Liberty Avenue remained untainted in my mind. I continued to revere our happy, friendly, peaceful days . . . in what had been for me a special and safe little enclave.

I love the country song that Miranda Lambert sings, "The House That Built Me." It reminds me of my childhood. Yet it was not a house, but a neighborhood, that built me. The one on Liberty Avenue in Rochester in the 1950s . . . caring, warm, close-knit, friendly. The best kind of place in which to grow up.

There is another song, one I composed myself at age eight, to the tune of "Knick Nack Paddy Wack":

> 313 Liberty
> Hopkins 7-6333
> That is the place for me
> 313 Liberty

It turned out that the veneer of serenity which clad the 1950s kindled the flaming eruptions of the '60s and beyond, not just in my family and neighborhood, but in the country as a whole, searing the pages of those parallel histories for all time.

Time Out

$\mathcal{T}$he recollections of a life are never linear, nor absolute. Neither can be their story. Yet sometimes to understand the life or its story, structuring is needed — a road map or timeline. And thus, I have constructed one which frames the external context of my life, both geographically and in time, to the best of my recollection and record . . . minus those details which would spoil the telling of things to come. This framework is included in the Appendix to this memoir, to which you may refer if you are, or become, confused about the who, what, when and where of my story. It is within that structure that my tale, and that of my family, unfolded. Some of the events have been revealed already. The Appendix should further illuminate those. Other happenings are yet to be told.

I hope this roadmap — the Appendix to which I refer — will allay confusion about when and where the remainder of my story unfolds. May you use it to your advantage. And now, back to the story.

Golden Rule Days

For fifty-five consecutive years, I loved school. And now, I treasure the memories.

School . . . where my foundation was poured. Where the fortifying walls of my being were erected. Where the bookends of my psyche were affixed. Growing up with a home life like a roller-coaster ride, school was my anchor.

School . . . those shiny hallways, filmy blackboards, dandruffy erasers. That dusky, disinfectanty smell. The prickle of anticipation every August as days shortened, nights cooled, and cicadas chirped their back-to-school melodies. School meant straight rows, regular routines, clear expectations, the good old golden rule.

School . . . that singular place where I found steadfast boundaries. From life in Missouri to New York, back again and beyond, school was my safe space. As a student, teacher, and principal — those walls of brick and mortar fortified my

81

being.

I entered kindergarten at Horace Mann Elementary School in Kansas City, where our roller coaster family had paused for a brief time. I remember my neighbor, Teddy, with his cozy name and brushy haircut, who liked to pull my blond pigtails. When Teddy visited, we played "Ebb Tide" on a portable keyboard on the front porch. He and I would belt out the odd lyrics as we hunted for the right keys. With music by numbers, we could play in harmony.

Most everything I remember about Kindergarten feels harmonious. However, the congruence I recall from school doesn't infuse my recollections of life at my grandparents' house that year, where my mother cried herself to sleep in the tiny bedroom we shared. My father was absent most of the time. My grandfather worked late shifts, so I rarely saw him, and my grandmother clucked and fretted at the sight of me.

In my entire school career, I only got in trouble two times. The first was in kindergarten. My classmate's cat had a new litter of kittens. How could I NOT stop to snuggle with them after school? I knew my phone number and wanted to call and tell my family where I was, but the friend's mother would not hang up. I must have stayed a long while. As I walked home, the kids along the way said, "You are in really big trouble."

My eyes widened at the sight of a police car in front of my grandparents' house. I noted that no one looked happy when I showed up, though my tearful mother did hug me hard before my grandmother extracted me. She whisked me up to that tiny bedroom.

"You did a very bad thing, not coming home on time," Grandma said. She was red in the face. "Everybody was worried."

My grandmother pronounced that the police had been about to dig into the deep snow pile on the playground which had fallen from the roof, thinking I might be trapped in there. She said that, when my friend's mother wouldn't let me use the phone, I should have gone straight home.

"You made a bad choice." She frowned.

Banished from the dinner table that night, I ate alone from a little tray my mother sneaked up the stairs to me.

The next day at school we heard lectures from a policeman about never doing what I had done. I would have said it was humiliating if I had known the word. Above all, I felt bad about having made my mother cry. Beginning at the tender age of five, I was already feeling the weight of responsibility for Mother's happiness. But I was also learning that if I did the right thing, school was a happy place for me.

Living in Kansas City didn't last. The roller coaster took us to Rochester, New York, where my father had landed a job as a newspaper reporter. I enrolled at Abraham Lincoln Elementary School . . . a small building of warm-looking, rusty red bricks where fearless teachers took their students out for recess on even the most daunting of winter days. How I loved those snowy play times! After recess, the classroom radiators hissed and clanked, draped as they were with smelly woolen socks, drippy scarves and sodden mittens. When I became a teacher, many years later, I felt guilty every time I declared an indoor recess because of the weather outside. Those hearty upstate New York teachers of my youth would have had none of that.

I adored my first-grade teacher, Mrs. Porries, the only elementary school teacher whose name I remember — as I do her curly, brown hair and warm, brown eyes. When we lined up to say goodbye at the end of the day, I kissed Mrs. Porries — that is, until my mother said I shouldn't.

The year was 1954. Without understanding what was happening, my classmates and I became Polio Pioneers. Quaking, we stood in line, waiting for the nurse to give us shots several times that year. The next year, some of us, including me, had to have the painful injections all over again. At little Abraham Lincoln Elementary, we were a part of the 1.8 million children across the United States, Canada and Finland, who were the human subjects for the research of Dr. Jonas Salk. A year later, Dr. Salk and his researchers announced that the vaccine was safe and effective for all children everywhere . . . too late for some, but a miracle for the future. Though I can no longer find my Polio Pioneer card, I feel pride in knowing that I was part of this crucial project. Many years later, myself a school administrator, I marveled that this research was ever conducted . . . with live human subjects . . . children, at that. Unimaginable in today's times.

In those years, another public-school practice that would be unthinkable today was when we Catholic students were dismissed early to attend religious instruction at Annunciation Church in preparation for First Communion.

"It's not fair!" our Protestant classmates said.

They must have thought we were having fun. They

didn't know our burly priest and how our lips quivered when he mounted the pulpit high above us. In scary terms, he condemned sin and spoke about forgiveness through confession. The nuns taught us what to do and say in the confessional, including what sins to relate. Just the thought of all this caused me to lose sleep at night. I racked my brain thinking up misdeeds to confess. Pulling the cat's tail? Turning down the corner on a page of my library book?

I survived that solitary ordeal in the small, dim booth with the gruff priest on the other side of a squeaking wooden screen. So did the others, and we emerged into the light of a white and beautiful First Communion celebration. After that, we did not have to leave Abraham Lincoln School early anymore, and I was glad.

My young heart was light at Abraham Lincoln school those two years — I was Cinderella, after all — solidifying my affinity for anything having to do with "education."

At the end of second grade, my family moved to our own house on Liberty Avenue, three miles away. I transferred to the shiny and sprawling Durand-Eastman School, where my third-grade teacher took a fondness to me. She didn't have children of her own and asked my mother if I could spend the night at her house one night. It was curious to me that she would make such a request — and that my parents, ignoring my discomfort at the prospect, would agree. At dinner with my teacher and her husband, my tongue was tied. The bedroom was pink and chilly. I squirmed all night. The term "teacher's pet" came to mind, and not in a good way. But I loved third grade and had fun every day except once when I collected fifty tiny cottonwood seeds and forgot them in my desk. Over the night, they popped open. The next morning when I lifted the top of the desk, fifty filmy orbs floated out and wafted all around the room. I was not the teacher's pet that day.

After school, my friends and I stayed for Brownie Scouts. The building was the same, but the rules were different. Some kids were unruly, and sometimes — guilty or not — we all got scolded or punished. And the Protestant Scouts didn't seem to like the Catholic ones. They made fun of us because we weren't allowed to go into the Lutheran Church at the start of the Fourth of July parade. Catholics could not enter Protestant churches, so we young Catholic Scouts had to wait on the front steps, joining the parade when the others came out. When I finished Brownies, I didn't want to "fly up" to be a Girl Scout, in part because they went to sleepover camp in the summer and I was afraid of that. Who would keep my mother company if I went away? Mother's brow was often furrowed. Maybe she would even move back to Kansas City with her family while I was gone. I skipped camp and never flew up.

Instead, the roller-coaster ride started up again. Both Mother and I ended up moving to Kansas City when my parents got their divorce. At the time, I didn't know what the word meant. Later, I would come to realize that divorce was a weighty stone cast into a pond, creating concentric circles that engulfed people for a lifetime.

My school life changed almost as dramatically as my home life did in the wake of that divorce. With no recollection of fifth grade at all, I was back in Kansas City where I ended up in a formidable school on the outskirts of the city, six blocks from my grandparents' house in which we were boarders once again. I needed school more than ever then, with my father gone and my mother consumed with tears, doctors, medications, and hospitalizations.

I had come to Kansas City, a product of the advanced suburban schools in Rochester, academically far ahead of my new urban classmates. The principal recommended I skip a grade, but I didn't . . . a wise decision given my fragile state at that time. Though, with repetitive lessons that did nothing to challenge me, I could have climbed inside my desk to get through each sorry day.

In time I made a friend, Jane, who had a thick, long brown pigtail down her back and was in my reading group. Jane had a beautiful singing voice. Like an angel, she sang in the descant section of the mandatory all-school chorus. There were only eight descants in the entire school. I longed to sit beside her in chorus.

"Ask the teacher," said Jane. "Go ahead, just ask."

I got up the nerve to talk to our teacher, telling him that singing the soprano notes made my throat sore. They were too low.

The teacher frowned and stared. My heart skipped a beat. But then his head tilted and turned. He looked at me out of the corner of his narrowed eyes.

"Okay, Nancy. You can sing with the descants."

Following that talk, the teacher let me clean the erasers at the end of the day. He assigned me to the Safety Patrol, after which the class bully stopped chasing and trapping me against the rough stone playground wall at recess. The bully's friend, Carlos, even gave me a chunky ring with a golden "C" on the black plastic "stone." Mother made me give it back.

In sixth grade, though the academics were repetitive, other learnings were far more enduring than the lessons in my textbooks: taming a hostile environment, making strategic friendship selections, winning the favor of a callous teacher, outsmarting threatening classmates. And the discovery that I am really an alto, not a descant.

The roller coaster climbed again, and I was off to suburbia once more, to the community of Raytown, a near-eastern suburb of Kansas City. There I entered the Raytown Junior High School. Life at home, beyond the sturdy brick walls of school, was precarious—no father, and a mother whose shaky steps to independence were headed for disaster. I immersed myself in the exhilaration of junior high life, making top grades and good friends in seventh grade. One of them was the person I would marry many years later. Unlike home, school was an environment which uplifted me.

My academic talents and preferences solidified. I loved reading, diagramming sentences and writing stories. But, like many of my friends, I struggled in Mrs. Aikmus' Algebra class. She was a gray-haired woman with big jiggly arms and huge hands. Most of the time, we saw only her ample backside as she plotted mysteries like "parabolas" on the blackboard.

One day, crowded under a black-and-white TV in the school lobby, the student body observed the start of the Space Race, and an ominous admonition to buckle down in science and math. Even so, I do not remember that Mrs.

Aikmus ever turned to face us in class. Algebra remained as unfathomable to me as were John Glenn's ground-breaking earth orbits aboard the Mercury capsule, Friendship 7.

Our Civics teacher, Mr. C., had slick dark hair and a foreign accent. He made my skin crawl. When he kept sitting on the girls' laps in class, we planned a defense.

"Let's take our compasses to Civics," we said. "We can hold them in our laps with the sharp points up. That'll stop him."

Score one for survival skills. And for something useful from Algebra class.

Mr. C. got the message. Disgruntled, he told my friend Linda and me the only reason we liked the aspiring John Fitzgerald Kennedy was that he was Catholic. But that was wrong—we liked JKF because he was handsome.

In Home Economics, I learned to sew. The training came in handy since money for clothes was so tight in my family. I made outfits for myself in both high school and college. (A sorority sister once told me I looked just like a page from the Sears Roebuck catalog). The Home Ec. teacher also tried teaching us to cook, but all I learned was not to wipe a broken egg off a hot stove surface. Oh, and not to eat the chocolate-chip cookie dough. That lesson didn't take.

Such were the chuckles and challenges of junior high. I tried to close my eyes to what was happening at home. I made good grades, found treasured friends, and became a cheerleader. As ninth grade came to an end, I was elated at the prospect of moving on to Raytown High School for tenth, eleventh, and twelfth grades. Home life was frugal and Mother was fragile, making some poor choices. But school was an escape—my reward.

Things didn't turn out the way they were supposed to. Once again, the roller-coaster intervened. We moved against my wishes, and I ended up having to go to the new and rival Raytown South High School for tenth grade, despite a failed ploy which involved listing a false address on the enrollment form. The RSHS principal said I was off to a poor start lying about my address and he would be surprised if I succeeded at his school. My heart was broken at leaving Raytown, where I felt I was something and somebody. Yet I knew school would have to save me from the disasters unfolding at home, so I willed myself to focus— to work hard, make new friends, and prove the principal wrong. And to give my mother no cause to worry about me. She needed to be worrying about herself, like I was. I often felt like I was the adult in the house, by then.

Finally, the year ended. And, with luck on my side for a change, we moved back to the Raytown High attendance area. I re-enrolled at the school that was more like a home than my home was, with two years of high school remaining.

School days bustled with good friends and caring teachers. Mr. McGee taught me to love literature; Miss Krumseik taught me to write. I made the drill team and wrote for the school newspaper. There were pep rallies, games, club meetings. And, for a time, the roller coaster at home paused at the top, revealing a view that was happy and hopeful. I hugged tight—to home, my family, my school, my friends, and ... by senior year ... to that handsome football captain I had met in seventh grade. We went to the Homecoming Dances and Senior Prom together. Indeed, he would eventually become my husband.

In those last grounding years at Raytown High School, I knew I wanted to stay in school forever . . . I would become a teacher. A teacher who, unlike Mrs. Aikmus, would face her students each day, eager with anticipation for shared adventure. I would care and nurture like Mrs. Porries. Inspire like Mr. McGee. Impart skills like Miss Krumseik, that incomparable woman who first revealed I was a writer. I submitted a heartfelt story for an assignment in her class. It earned an A.

"This is excellent, Nancy. I want to publish it in the *Blue Horizons*."

Blue Horizons was our school's literary journal, produced annually by Miss Krumseik.

"Oh, no, Miss Krumseik," I said. "No one can read it. I would be too embarrassed. It was just for you to see."

"Then we can publish it anonymously."

And we did . . . my first-ever publication. That very story, then called "The Pogo Stick," lived in my head for fifty-five years, fuel for my yearning to write about my childhood. And now expanded, it is called "How to Learn That Winning Isn't Everything," and it resides on the pages of this, my long-delayed memoir

Emma Krumseik showed me that I could, and should, write. And that I would teach. Thus, by the end of high school, I knew I wanted to smell school, breathe school, live school—stable, firm, predictable—for all time.

My love of school sustained me through college and into advanced certifications and graduate degrees. I profited from all my lessons — positive and negative, academic and survival. Even the crusty RSHS principal had made a difference. When I became a principal myself, I made sure I learned every student's first name, greeted each of them at the door in the morning, and bade them goodbye in the afternoon. I was the head cheerleader for their achievements.

"How do you remember all our names?" the children would say. They hugged me and I hugged them back. No one ever called me crusty. At least, not to my knowledge.

When the bricks-and-mortar of my roller-coaster home life teetered, crumbled and caved for good, I survived the implosion. I know that many factors — caring people and just enough luck — imparted the strength to maintain my footing despite ever-shifting familial sands. Yet the essential elements of my foundation, the one that stands firm today, were poured in seven schools over twelve years.

I believe I always have been — and always will be — a student, a teacher, an educator. And that from within the fortifying walls of the schools I so loved, despite familial circumstances which conspired to topple them, my dreams ascended. So now, with the benefit of the lessons I learned, plus the extra credit of hindsight and life experience, those dreams boost me onto a roller coaster trip of my own conception. The one on which I ride today . . . at long last, recounting my story.

CLOUDING OVER

"A dysfunctional family is any family with more than one person in it."

Mary Karr

By the Silvery Light

*T*here was a full moon the night my childhood died. Underfoot, the grass felt as crisp and frosty as a crunchy bowl of sugared cereal. I watched my family traipse round and round the modest front yard of my aunt's little house . . . their feet blistering with the cold. Walking, dragging, staggering—supporting a limp and struggling figure—an adult Raggedy Ann doll. After what seemed like an eternity, an ambulance arrived. To a ten-year-old only child whose father had announced that he would soon leave and whose mother had just swallowed an entire bottle of sleeping pills, time stood still.

My mother and I were sleeping in different bedrooms on this strained visit to Missouri. She had crept into my room during the night—where I lay alone on the bottom bunk with someone, a cousin perhaps, asleep above. Mother placed her pallid hands on my cheeks, cradling my sleeping face. Disoriented and groggy, I roused to a blurred awareness.

Was I hearing her say goodbye? That she wouldn't be there the next morning? Something about pills? As I struggled to sit upright, I comprehended a weak and whispered declaration of love. Some part of these muffled messages caused my blood to run cold. I bolted from the bed.

I don't know what I did or said, but it roused the others in the house. They sprang into action.

Medics were called. Everyone took to the frosted lawn under that gleaming spotlight of a moon—some walking round and round—me frozen in the shadows. The idea, it seemed, was to keep Mother from going to sleep.

Someone said they would pump her stomach at the hospital and, if they did it quickly enough, she wouldn't die. I heard—processed—the word "die" for the first time. A frozen arrow of fear pierced the depths of my young soul.

She did not die that night . . . although the marriage did. The dreaded divorce came about. Amid my father's grim determination, my own helpless longing, and my mother's devastation, our family disbanded.

Mother and I were moved from our home in Rochester . . . installed into the house of my shell-shocked grandparents, in Kansas City. There were not enough bedrooms, so they put me on the enclosed back porch. Little warmth reached that spot, and I had few reserves of my own. Alone on the first floor, I faced the darkness wrapped in chilly tendrils of midnight, awash in tattered thoughts. When the full moon appeared, my solitary mind conjured a frosty evening on a frozen front lawn. Treasured memories of Rochester—two parents, a home, pets, friends—did nothing to warm me. No longer "Nancy with the Laughing Face," my eyes closed to the unbidden vision of a rusted red pogo stick abandoned in the corner of an empty garage.

Years later, we wondered . . . did I go to fifth grade in Rochester or Kansas City? No one seemed to know. Within frayed transplanted cardboard boxes, we found report cards, awards, and mementos from every other year in school. But not a single artifact from the lost year. The year when, under the searing light of a gleaming full moon, my childhood died.

Cousins

On a visit to see my sweet Kansas City cousins and their spunky Beagle, Sparky, there was a yet another new batch of puppies . . . squirmy newborn baby Beagles with their eyes not even open. On that afternoon, my cousins' dad filled a big silver bucket with water. I thought he might be watering the flowers—he was a dad that did those kinds of things.

"What are you doing, Uncle Jim?"

I called him my uncle though, in reality, he was a cousin too. He, his wife, and their kids—four girls and a boy, all younger than me—were my second and third cousins on my mother's side. I loved visiting this fun family and the friendly Sparky dog, who was usually expecting. Sparky might have been friendlier than she should have been—she became a mom so often.

"Too many puppies, too many times," Uncle Jim said,

with a deep frown. "Sparky wasn't supposed to have any more puppies. We can't take care of these."

That said, in front of all of us, he drowned the whole litter in that shining silver bucket. The shock almost took me to my knees. How could he do such a terrible thing? He was so nice, so gentle. I knew Jim was a good person, a good father, because his kids were happy when he was home. The puppy drownings caused me tears and nightmares, but that was nothing compared to what was to come for their family.

Uncle Jim worked for the railroad. We visited his railyard—I loved watching the trains and thinking how exciting it would be to hear the clickety-clack of those trains each day as they uncoupled and reconnected in the railyard. I thought of my father's Lionel train around our Christmas trees in the Rochester days. To this day, I am a fan of trains and train travel.

I had forgiven Uncle Jim for the puppies. He had an explanation of why the drowning was necessary, though the rationale escapes me now. I envied how their family laughed and loved each other. They made it look like fun having sisters and brothers to grow up with. And a loving father, of course. But then, Uncle Jim was killed in the railyard. On that day, his family's bubbly joy ended, and I learned that there was more than one way to lose a dad. And that every time, it changes everything.

"He didn't deserve to die," said my grieving mother. She loved Uncle Jim like I did. "But at least the kids will be taken care of with the railroad insurance money."

I never forgot that family . . . my sweet cousins, their puppies, their parents. The oldest of these cousins, Tony, has helped me to recall our times together. We live miles and miles from one another, and we still stay in touch, though not nearly often enough—mostly through the clichéd Christmas card and letter. Such is the way of many cousins . . . a shame.

I also had first cousins on my father's side—a boy and a girl—but like him, they disappeared from my life. I met them and their parents only once or twice when I was quite young. I know their names, Lynn and Dean; not much else. But I do wonder what happened to them and whether the surname Hill has died out by now. Those cousins became just two more missing pieces in the fragmented puzzle that was my childhood.

People say it's a shame to grow up without a lot of cousins, and that's probably true. I didn't have many, but there were two others who made up for that.

Cousin-in-Chief

"Watch my duck while I'm at school, Nancy. You're in charge. Make sure she has food and water and don't let anything happen to her." We stood beside the outdoor cage below my cousin's bedroom window. Two years my senior, Gretchen was my idol.

My six-year-old lips quivered at her explicit instructions. I yearned to be like her, to please her. Following the emphatic directive, she zipped off to catch the school bus, leaving me staring into the duck's cage with a thumping heart. We both knew the duck was suffering from diarrhea.

My mother, father and I had flown to Dallas to visit Aunt Julie, Uncle Max, and my cousins Gretchen and Gary. Some of my earliest memories of these first cousins, especially Gretchen, are from that trip. I would soon learn that, like her formidable mother, Gretchen—even at age eight—was a life force. She would grow up to play a major role in our family lore.

There was already water and food in the cage, and the duck wasn't doing much. I soon became bored, so I took a break to ride on the backyard swings. I loved to swing as high as I could go. At home in Rochester, I spent many a serene hour on my swings. I may have extended my duck-watching break too long. When I returned to the cage, I found the little duck lying on its back in the corner. I gasped and ran inside.

Aunt Julie and Mother came in a hurry. Always the commanding general, Julie took charge. We spent hours visiting farms that sold ducks. Around Dallas in those days, you could just go out and buy a duck whenever you needed one. We came across a tan and brown one that was almost identical to Gretchen's perished pet. Back at the house, Aunt Julie cleaned the cage and put the new duck in. It looked a little scrawny to me. I said a silent prayer.

With my heart in my throat, I watched Gretchen get off the school bus. She raced to see her duck. The little thing pecked happily about. It had pooped in one corner of the cage.

"That's not my duck! It's too small, and it doesn't have diarrhea!"

Gretchen stormed into the house. When the truth came out, she insisted we return the bogus duckling. She wanted no part of it. I don't remember what happened to the doomed little duck, but I ached inside, having let my idol down.

When I first saw my cousins' house in suburban Dallas, I thought it was glamorous. Tawny wood cabinets and rust-colored patterned linoleum adorned the warm, glowing kitchen. There was a living room and a family room with a brick fireplace. We didn't have a family room or a fireplace in Rochester, and I wondered why. A fire would have come in handy in those frosty upstate New York winters.

Earlier that year, Gretchen had made her first Holy Communion. She liked to play nun. She and I draped ourselves with sheets and put rosaries around our waists. We built an altar in her bedroom to serve communion using Necco wafers. When I was lucky, I got one of the chocolate ones. Gretchen taught me prayers and hymns. I thought she would grow up to be a nun, but that didn't happen. Far from it.

It came time for us to leave. On the way to the airport, in the back seat of the car, I bounced back and forth and twirled a long blond lock of hair around my finger. My father scowled at those nervous habits of mine, but I bounced and twirled and bounced and twirled as we raced to catch our plane. We missed it. He told me it was my fault.

"Every time you bounced back, Nancy, it made the car go backwards. That's what caused us to be late." I sensed the hint of a smile in his words. I smiled, too, because we got to stay another day.

Gretchen and I set up a vet office in the basement. Her gentle Cocker Spaniel, Kaycee, yelped as we lifted him onto the ping-pong table and stuck him with play syringes all afternoon. By the end of the day, he had splints on his legs and sticky bandages on his paws. We named our clinic the Greenhill Veterinary after our last names, Green and Hill.

We promised we would become vets and open a Greenhill Clinic when we grew up. Gretchen should have done that. She ended up raising many dogs ... pets and hunting companions, well-bred and well-trained. Except for Red, her Irish Setter, who stole thawing tenderloin steaks right off the kitchen counters. Red was a devil dog, mischievous but loyal to a fault. Red adored Gretchen, and Gretchen adored her. Though neither of us became veterinarians, my cousin and I always shared a love of dogs.

Though brusque Aunt Julie and outspoken Gretchen could overwhelm me back then, I loved Uncle Max without reservation. In his crisp Air Force uniform, he stood tall and erect, his blond crew cut hidden beneath a stiff cap. He looked stern, but his eyes twinkled, and he had a warm smile. I remember his gentle voice.

Sometime later, I heard my mother tell my father that Aunt Julie wanted a divorce from that good man. She said Julie wanted a bigger house and more money. I don't know if that was true, or if Uncle Max even knew about it, but I will never forget the phone call that came to us in Rochester one day.

Uncle Max was dead. They found him in that tawny kitchen with a gun in his hand and a bullet in his head. My cousin Gary was at work at his first job in a grocery store. He learned of his father's death when a priest came to the store to tell him. The priest took Gary home.

Mother gasped for breath at the news about Uncle Max. She couldn't stop sobbing. A deep frown creased my father's brow above a grave look in his eyes. I felt icy fingers squeeze my heart; the pressure in my chest made it hard to breathe. A father gone; a family torn apart. I cried for Uncle Max and at the thought of my cousins living without a father, thankful to have a father of my own. I knew nothing of what was to come.

After Uncle Max died, Aunt Julie, Gretchen and Gary moved back to Kansas City where our grandparents lived.

"I don't remember much of anything until after we moved to Kansas City," Gary now says. Like I do, Gary draws some blanks from his memory bank.

Unlike Gretchen, Gary — seven years my senior — was not a regular presence in my life, but I remember him as tan and golden. When in high school, he drove a red Triumph TR3, had handsome teenage friends, and soon — like his father before him — donned an Air Force uniform. I didn't keep in touch with Gary after he went off to the military, but he grew into the spitting image of our grandfather — minus the plugs of snuff — and cooking as well as Grandpa Robb did. He ended up living in Hawaii — with his wife, children, and grandchildren — and visiting annually in Kansas City. He still cooks legendary dishes. Though we are far apart in miles, we remain close in heart and communication.

As things turned out, it was my mother, not Aunt Julie, who got the divorce. And like my cousins, I was fatherless too. As a result, Mother and I also moved to Kansas City. We lived at my grandparents' house once again. Gretchen, Gary and Aunt Julie lived not far away, in Raytown. We had all lost a lot, but — for a while — we had each other.

This time, I slept not on my grandparents' chilly back porch, but in a tiny bedroom on the second floor. Its only remarkable feature was a window dormer onto a steep, sloping front-porch roof.

"We're going out that window to the roof," Gretchen said one afternoon, with a glint in her eye. Even as a young teen, she could cook up some world-class schemes. Sometimes she succeeded in recruiting me to join her.

On our daring roof-scaling day, Gretchen and I climbed out and curled up like stealthy kittens. My legs trembled. Especially when—from under her sweatshirt—Gretchen produced a bottle of Mogen David wine. We snickered, whispered, and sipped. This first forbidden sampling of wine tasted sweet and tangy. We surveyed the sweeping view and tried to spot our parents' alma mater, Paseo High School, on a hill in the distance. After a few more swigs of wine, my knees stopped knocking. This was feeling a bit like fun.

But then the window flew open. We paled at the sight of a red-faced Aunt Julie. How had she figured out where we were, what we were doing? Our illicit adventure came to a halt when, like runaway sheep, we were wrestled inside.

"Bend over," she said. The brush was soft, but its memory still stings. I cried, but my impudent cousin didn't even flinch.

I never ventured onto the roof again, with or without Gretchen. Nor did I develop a taste for Mogen David wine or secret shenanigans. In my mind, Gretchen's gleaming halo had begun to lose some of its shine.

While I stuck to the straight and narrow, Gretchen continued to be a renegade. As a teenager, with her many friends and boyfriends, she dove from dangerous cliffs at

Lake Jacomo, not far from Raytown. There were reports that alcohol was involved. And smoking. The Jacomo cliffs were not the last of Gretchen's rebellious acts in life. She went on to marry the wrong man, suffer the effects of a gruesome divorce, and lose custody of her first-born child. But she weathered those drastic years, coming out of them with a beloved second child, Andrew, who idolized her, and says she would have been an awesome grandmother.

I'm not sure when I realized since neither of us had sisters upon which to inflict terror, Gretchen and I developed our own love-hate relationship. She could be the queen of mean — it hurt when she wouldn't let me have her outgrown clothes or, at the junior high pep rally, didn't give me credit for helping her and her upperclassmen friends write the first-ever school anthem. I wonder if the RJHS students still sing 'Nestled in a valley yonder . . .' that I helped to compose — my first published piece of writing.

My cousin and I shared meanness, laughter, and love in equal parts. If she could, I'm sure Gretchen would relate injustices of my doing as well.

Like two roads diverging in a wood, we followed dramatically different paths. I couldn't have chosen a more opposite route. While she flamed through marriage, divorce, affairs and more . . . I played the role of dedicated student and devoted girlfriend who went steady, became lavaliered, pinned, engaged and married . . . all to the same man, my high school boyfriend. I craved stability while she lived to push beyond the envelopes of life.

In some ways, Gretchen and I mirrored the relationship between Aunt Julie and my mother. The three of them were the most relevant women of my early life, and I have thought of the four of us in a boat together:

—Aunt Julie at the helm, in full-dress uniform, barking orders . . .

—Mother scurrying to carry out Julie's directives, fretting over everyone's safety, suffering in silence . . .

—Me in the stern, flotation jacket riveted in place, teeth clenched, making sure not to rock the boat . . .

—And Gretchen on the prow, arms outstretched, rocking with abandon, caring not that she might perish . . . or capsize us all.

We loved, we hated . . . but always . . . we laughed. There was a legendary party around Gretchen's hot tub one icy Kansas City New Year's Eve. Gretchen's naked friend fell and froze to the ice on the deck at the back of the house. The woman's husband, racing to meet the ambulance, slid down the front porch steps. They both ended up with broken legs. One would think a few scrapes and bruises would have been enough. Though drastic at the time, this story provided years of family laughter. I only wish I had been there to see it, like so many of Gretchen's other escapades. Burning her candle at both ends.

There was a Christmas when, with the entire family around a twinkling tree, I unwrapped Gretchen's gift . . . to reveal a box labeled 'Computer Mouse'. I can still hear my blood-curdling scream as a live mouse scampered out and went straight up my arm.

Back then, our adult Christmases were liberally laced with sparkling Cold Duck and Gretchen's matchless blender creation—her famous 'Lemon Swizzles'. Such hilarious holiday memories—though I haven't had a glass of Cold Duck or a Swizzle since.

I find I am left with fewer memories of the meanness and anger and greater recollections of laughter and love. And now, the sorrow.

Those times we wrapped up in bedsheets, playing nun and giving Communion, did not bring Gretchen a slice of immortality. Though it is fun to pretend that there was once a day when a rosary fit around my waist, that memory does not offset my cousin's cruel fate.

I regret I can never repay Gretchen for the love and care she devoted to my mother in her darkest hours. None of us could slay Mother's demons, but my cousin's efforts were valiant.

I wince at the memory of our last hours together, when I washed and massaged her ravaged fifty-eight-year-old feet ... feet which had led Gretchen into so many dangerous deeds but ended up delivering her to the final agonizing weeks of pancreatic cancer. I so hope she went to her grave wearing the searing red toenail polish I applied. And I pray that she, with scarlet toes and her devil-dog Red at her side, is blazing through eternity, lighting the sky in her wake.

Rest in peace my cousin-in-chief, sister from another mother. If I had my way, we would be on a rooftop somewhere, cracking open a bottle of Cold Duck or downing a batch of Lemon Swizzles. Laughing. And swapping grandchildren stories, of course.

Family Democracy

$\mathcal{T}$he two yappy Chihuahuas barked and nipped. I jerked away from those alarming little dogs as we jostled into our seats at this family feast of guampkies and peroghis. The occasion was a raucous winter dinner at the Chronopoulis house. The well-laden tables were set . . . adults in the dining room and kids in the kitchen . . . each room diffusing mouthwatering aromas and cheerful chatterings. Mogen David wine flowed freely around the adult table. The decibel levels grew.

Nine short years in my muted triad of a family in New York had done little to prepare me for the shock of becoming part of this rowdy, multigenerational, multiethnic extended family in Kansas City. Sometimes it seemed like my mother and I were from a different planet—one much quieter, repressed. At this dinner, in addition to those unruly dogs, the principals were:

—Grandmother Zella, who could speak both Polish and English, but seemed more comfortable not speaking much at all. When she wasn't unnerved or annoyed by my cousins and me, she tried to teach us odd Polish words. She told us that, had the family stayed in Poland, we would be royalty—Polish princes and princesses. I liked the thought of being a princess and wondered about life in Poland. Maybe my grandmother had liked it better there.

—Grandfather Julius, the hearty, jovial Hungarian, with his chaws of tobacco and big, sloppy kisses. We hated those messy kisses then; I would give a million dollars for one now.

—Polish-speaking Aunt Jenny, Zella's effusive sister, and her lusty Greek husband, Uncle Mike Chronopoulis. Aunt Jenny always called us funny-sounding Polish names. She smiled and laughed as she chased and grabbed us to smother our faces with kisses. I wasn't used to being hugged and kissed with such vigor. Now I wish I hadn't tried so hard to escape.

—My mother, Violet, and her only sibling, my Aunt Julie. Two sisters, each both Polish and Hungarian. As different as night is from day. Mother, Grandmother Zella's clone. Julie, the essence of Grandfather Julius.

—And the kids—my cousins Gretchen and Gary, and me; our patchwork bloodlines intermingled with those of our fathers, whatever those might have been. I remember Aunt Jenny and Uncle Mike's daughters, too, but not on the occasion in question.

Among these folks, on that unforgettable evening, sat Aunt Julie's friend—a tall, dark, curly-headed Italian—Tony

Pika.

At our table in the kitchen, we kids could make out only bits of the conversation in the dining room. But we didn't miss it when a heavy fist hit the table, followed by Uncle Mike's accented roar.

"Everybody downstairs. We going to settle this once and for all."

The suddenly silenced family filed onto the basement stairs. My face reddened as I spotted damp underwear hanging from a clothesline stretched across one corner. A sturdy wooden ironing board sat next to a washer, dryer, and laundry tub. A menacing ringer-type washer loomed large, like the one in my grandmother's basement. I knew to stay away from that . . . it could rip off an arm. Braided rag throw rugs like the one I had napped on in kindergarten were scattered about. Under bare lightbulbs, the adult faces looked angry or blank. My teeth chattered.

About twelve at the time, I was still struggling to adjust to Mother's post-divorce life in Kansas City. She and I resided in cramped quarters with my grandparents. My aunt and cousins lived in nearby Raytown. The youngest of the brood, I was still a relative newcomer—not yet desensitized to the family antics.

"You kids sit on stairs. Everybody else against wall."

Uncle Mike's accent did not diminish the intensity of this directive. As judge and jury, he towered in front of the group of adults—some shivering, others fuming. His back was to us on the stairs, but we could see the expressions on all the others' faces. If I had known the phrase, I would have said there was an elephant in the room.

"Okay. There is big problem in this family. Max has been gone only few years. Now Julie has taken up with Tony Pika here. But we are all good Catholics."

The logic made little sense to me. My widowed aunt worked at TWA, where she had met the dashing airline pilot named Tony. I liked him and I thought Gretchen and Gary did, too. But in that basement, Tony's ever-friendly, cheerful countenance eclipsed as he stood at the center of the family group, next to my red-faced aunt.

Uncle Mike continued.

"This is big problem. Causing too much trouble. Julie and Tony say they love each other, but what about Tony's wife and kids in New Jersey? Do they love this? Good Catholics don't break up marriage. And divorce is sin. We know this."

Like an electric shock, this pronouncement jolted me. I didn't know Tony Pika was married. I peeked toward my newly divorced mother. With bowed head and lifeless eyes, she stared at the floor.

"This relationship—this love—between Julie and Tony is sin." After that proclamation, Uncle Mike continued. "We will give Julie, Tony, anybody else who wants to talk a chance. Right now. Then we are going to vote."

Vote? Vote on what? Who was going to vote? Me?

My breath caught in my chest. Things never used to happen this way when my mother, father, and I lived together in New York. With us, things had been silent, private, unstated. There was never any voting on our fate. If there had been, I would have voted against their divorce.

While I remember little of what was said in that

basement, the visual tableau is fixed in my memory. Tall, dark Tony with his arm around Aunt Julie, the harsh light igniting her blond hair and flaming green eyes. My mother staring at the floor. Aunt Jenny, wringing her hands as if twisting laundry. Grandmother Zella, moaning into her handkerchief. My grandfather rooted like a mighty oak illuminated in a bolt of lightning.

We kids were statues on the stairs ... Gary and Gretchen's features frozen, unreadable. I remember thinking that I would like for Tony to be my uncle, but it would be bad for his wife and children. Their family would be all torn apart like mine was.

It didn't take long for the speeches, if there were any. It was time to vote.

"Go stand by Tony and Julie if you want them to get married. Otherwise, stand by me. Adults only."

Uncle Mike glared. Upon hearing "adults only," I breathed again.

I don't remember who stood where—or what else happened that night—but I still recall those yapping Chihuahuas. I couldn't stand those dogs. They were far more difficult to take than was my chaotic new family. At least the adults didn't bite.

Aunt Julie and Tony Pika did not get married.

Not long after the bizarre voting evening, Julie began dating Joe, a rich man who did business with TWA. Oil was involved. Joe was not a Catholic; Gary and Gretchen called him "The Sheik." Despite his reported wealth, he gave us underwear and socks for Christmas. Aunt Julie married him and moved to Saudi Arabia. Gary dropped out of college and joined the Air Force. Gretchen was sent to boarding school in Switzerland.

Mother and I moved into Aunt Julie's house in Raytown. I liked that we had a house to live in on our own, but then Gretchen ran away from the Swiss boarding school and, when they tracked her down, she was sent back home to live with us. She was always in a bad mood and refused to let me have her outgrown clothes, even though they didn't fit her anymore.

I fumed. "Gretchen, you will never wear these things again!"

"I don't care. They're mine—not yours."

Thus, my dreams of wearing a camel-hair coat to junior high school came to an end. Much later, I realized that Gretchen's dreams must have been dying then, too.

Somehow having divorced "The Sheik," Aunt Julie returned to Raytown. Mother and I had to find somewhere else to live.

As a young teenager, I didn't know what to think of this family or how to make my way within it. Though I was too young to heed them, alarm bells must have been going off in my head. I felt lost.

More family dramas were to follow. Over the years, I witnessed alcohol and guns, infidelities and divorces, pregnancies and the ends of them. Family members leaving their homes and moving in with others, only to move back home again. Siblings not speaking for years. Arguments, threats, estrangements, recriminations, reconciliations. Toward the end of high school, I resolved I would never permit such scenarios in my own adult life. Despite tough personal choices and collateral damages, it was a promise I kept.

Nature or Nurture?

*P*eople sometimes debate the implications of nature versus nurture. In my mind, there is no debate at all. I come down solidly on the side of nature. That's not a reflection upon the nurturing I have known or not known. Rather, this conviction comes from my life experiences. Specifically, with cooking . . . cooking as a nurtured skill as opposed to having the "cooking gene."

My first memories of food, of cooking, come from Rochester—where my mother, father, and I lived until I was in fourth grade. (Or fifth grade, but that's a different story.) I can picture our kitchen and the sink below a curtained window, framing my much-loved swing set. I see the refrigerator. I remember a wall oven with a timer—a ticking device that my father turned on to measure my occasional timeouts. I can even feel the hard seat of the oaken timeout stool in the corner. Yet I cannot picture a stove . . . nor anyone in front of one. I know, though, that my mother was our only cook. And that she must have worked hard at it, like she did most everything she undertook. Though my mind's eye no longer replays the culinary sequences, I have to think that my mother cooked with dedication and care. However, some critical elements may have been lacking: budget perhaps, gratification probably, appreciation no doubt. Like other aspects of Mother's life during those years.

I can conjure up the sights and smells of some regular meals: fish sticks, tuna casserole, toasted cheese with canned tomato soup — staples in our house. Oh, and canned salmon fashioned into patties, with those suspicious, squishy round bones that were "good for you." There is an aromatic memory of pot roast now and then, and liverwurst sandwiches with mayonnaise, though never on Fridays. Yes, we were Catholic.

What I remember most were the peas . . . and gagging in front of those smelly little green beads. Sitting at the table, staring at peas until bedtime. Rolling the horrid things around my plate. Trying to balance them on my knife. All to the tune of that common mantra of the time — "think of those starving children in China." My father insisted upon clean plates. I'm not sure how I ever got to leave the table for bed on pea nights, because I did everything but eat them. No doubt, my mother intervened.

These early gastronomic scenarios probably did not nurture much love in my young psyche . . . for eating, for cooking, certainly not for peas. I outgrew two of those issues.

Then came my parents' divorce, which landed me in the Midwest amid a big ethnic extended family. The patriarch was my grandfather, Julius Robb. I soon learned that he was a world-class cook. Despite having grown up in the hard-scrabble coal mining towns of western Pennsylvania, he somehow ended up in Kansas City and, by the time I got there, was the head chef at the iconic downtown hotel, the Muehlebach. Grandpa worked late and didn't drive, so on many evenings, we picked him up after dark. We thrilled at the sight of his generous overcoat pockets bulging with filets, T-bones, lobster tails and the like. Such a great perk of his chef's position. He even amassed, one bottle at a time, a stash of champagne for my wedding — with a limited budget, it was the only champagne we could provide our guests. Grandpa Robb, the kind-hearted chef, the culinary legend in the family, the man for whom, years later, one of my sons was named. Julius Robb . . . indisputable evidence of the cooking gene's presence in our clan.

The various family kitchens in Kansas City were crowded with cooks. Usually all women. In the background sat my great-grandmother, Grandma Pater. She spoke Polish, only Polish, and had no teeth. While not engaged in the cooking, per se, she kept up a running stream of mutterings in apparent judgment of what everyone else was doing. Now and then, she would rise from her chair to grab a wooden spoon and shake it at someone. No doubt she possessed the cooking gene, though it may have gone dormant by the time I knew her.

Her daughter, Zella Robb — my grandmother, the

reigning matriarch—hovered at the edge of the scene, chopping things at the table, now playing the role of revered sous chef. The central character, the taskmaster, was my mother's sister, Zella's other daughter . . . the formidable Aunt Julie. Like a whirling dervish, she whipped from task to task and dish to dish. She barked orders to the others. She scrubbed every surface before anyone knew it was dirty, brandishing what was known as her ever-present "Polish rag." In cooking, as in all matters, Julie cracked the family whip.

My mother, whose cooking gene had apparently been dormant in New York, rose to the challenge. She began cooking like a champ. Also, often at Julie's side, were my cousins Gretchen and Gary, rounding out four generations of cooks performing their craft. These were crowded, frenetic scenes for a timid, transplanted ten-year-old consumed, not with learning to cook, but with wishing her life could go back to the way it had always been. Except, maybe, for the meals.

Sometimes, when I felt brave, I ventured a peek into those raucous kitchens. Grumbling and vibrating upon the stove sat a steaming chrome pressure cooker. Out of that beast emerged melt-in-the-mouth guampkies, no doubt bringing posthumous pride to ancient Polish ancestors. Over the years, countless heads of cabbage and vast paddies of rice were sacrificed at the altar of those guampkies. Or— there were the times when our meals were Hungarian, in tribute to Grandpa Robb's heritage—thick, bubbling meaty goulashes whose aromas alone would bring one to tears. Or the pungent oxtail stew, the mere mention of which causes my mouth to water yet today.

And then there were the legendary fried chicken feasts. I made sure to stay a safe distance away during the cooking of those, with the attendant pops, crackles, hissings, and shrieks of "ye Gods," or "Oy gevalt!" Those dinners — that crispy fried chicken and thick creamy gravy ladled over fluffy mashed potatoes dripping with golden butter — were over-the-top delicious, even when the cooks came to the table bearing blisters on their arms, hands, or faces.

Such were the Kansas City culinary scenes to which I was introduced. Never did a fish stick or canned salmon patty dare to appear in those aromatic galleys. Rarely did I, either — myself an uncomfortable fifth wheel in the vigorous venues. My cousins Gretchen and Gary not only joined the fray, but paid attention. They both grew up to be accomplished cooks in the Robb tradition. And then there was me.

Fast-forward to the summer of 1968, that golden season of my engagement. My mother made a proclamation.

"Everyone in this family is an excellent cook, Nancy," she said, looking at me with a raised eyebrow. My mother's eyebrows were thick and lush. I took notice. "Before you get married, you are going to learn to cook. You owe it to John."

Mother loved John. She might have been worried about his nutritional future. Or perhaps she thought back to her own days as a young cook in Rochester . . . hoping to spare John a similar early marriage scenario.

And thus, Mother invited John to dinner every Wednesday evening that summer. Regardless of her motives, I approved. Not that I looked forward to the cooking lesson, but I loved any excuse for a mid-week date and, better yet, a harmonious time around the dinner table with my family.

Mother meant business. She and I planned menus and made lists. While shopping together, she gave me tips about item selection. We bought fresh vegetables, potatoes, cheeses, and proteins, though there was no such term back then. For us, proteins were big Kansas City steaks, lobster tails, shrimp, and huge pork chops for stuffing. The cash register went *cha-ching*. Mother wrote out the checks. I remained oblivious to costs, but I recognized the complexities of putting a "mere meal" on the table. My admiration for my mother grew. My affinity for cooking did not.

On Wednesdays, we worked hard. I enjoyed setting the table better than preparing the meal, but I stayed close by Mother's side. With infinite patience, she explained each step, noting in writing every minute detail. Those notes formed the start of my recipe collection. Some of them exist to this day — on stained, yellowed paper scraps in my recipe box, in my mother's distinctive, spidery handwriting.

A great deal of careful, individualized nurturing comprised those Wednesday feasts. The dinners were delicious. John was appreciative and — most likely — hopeful. Other than the week when a wine glass shattered and Mother had to be taken for stitches, it was all pretty perfect. I felt an appreciation for my mother that had been dormant for years.

John and I married in late August and honeymooned in Daytona Beach, driving there from Kansas City after the wedding. Mother presented a pain-filled smile at our departure. After the trip, we headed back north to our first apartment, a tiny one-bedroom student abode in Columbia, Missouri, where we were finishing degrees at the University. We had prepared the apartment in advance, decorated in trendy turquoise and olive green. A little metal-rimmed Formica table loomed at the edge of the combined living/dining room, as if daring me to fill it. I had already set it with pride—unveiling our sparkling new Blue Willow china, just waiting for that first home-cooked meal.

"I need to go to the bank for a few hours," John said, after we had unpacked. He worked part time at a local bank.

"Okay, I'll drive you there. Then I can go to the store for stuff to make dinner." As students, we were grateful to have a car of our own . . . a shiny new burgundy-colored Ford Fairlane . . . our wedding gift from John's parents.

I dropped my new husband off at the bank but didn't go to the store. In a mounting state of alarm, I hastened back to the apartment. From off the shelf, I snatched my brand-new, red-and-white checkered *Better Homes and Gardens* cookbook, a shower gift—from my mother, most likely. I scoured the Table of Contents, frowning. There came a knock on the door. It was a welcoming neighbor bringing us a warm and fragrant bundt cake.

"How sweet," she said. "The newlywed planning the first meal. What are you having?" She must have snickered to herself upon seeing me . . . a deer in the headlights.

I tried to sound undecided—rather than terrified at facing the sad recognition that, despite a summer of lessons, I had no idea what to cook or how to cook it.

"Um, not sure yet. But thanks so much for the dessert."

I hurried to the store and later picked John up at the bank. He hopped in the car and . . . grinning at the cliché . . . asked, "What's for dinner?"

His grin faded at my muttered reply, "Chili dogs."

Later, when our time as students ended, John made two culinary requests. No more chili dogs. And no tuna casseroles either, please. But, ever the diplomat, he never inquired about what became of the skills my mother had tried so valiantly to pass on.

So much for my cooking legacy. Despite intense nurturing, the genetic imprint skipped me. I am happy to report, however, that with no nurturing at all—quite the contrary—the capricious little culinary gene found its way to our future son, named Robb, after my grandfather. His brother, our other child, does a respectable job in the kitchen as well. In addition, both sons were blessed to inherit another gene. One that said to marry someone unlike their mother. Someone who can cook.

Nature vs. nurture . . . I rest my case.

ECLIPSE

"If you don't want to sink, you better figure out how to swim."

Jeannette Walls

When the Bough Broke

*M*y mother was in her mid-thirties when divorce darkened her world. She contended that the breakup was not of her making, nor was it something she wanted. I — the solitary offspring, a remnant of the failed marriage — became my mother's ten-year-old charge, part of her baggage as we shipped off from New York to Missouri.

Mother thought her life was over. She wanted it to be over. When she survived and found that it was not, she fell into a deep depression, saddled with the pain of her own existence. With a child to care for, at a time when she could not and did not wish to care for herself. Overwhelmed by her burdens, she succumbed to a dim existence of shock treatments, therapy sessions, medications. For weeks and months on end . . . for her, Hell on Earth. And for that ten-year-old charge . . . a world of disorientation, incomprehension, hurt.

Over time, Mother took steps toward wellness, independence. Out of necessity, she found a job. She and I ended our sequestration with my grandparents and, after a time in my aunt's temporarily vacant house, rented a place nearby in a complex called Raytown Gardens. We moved onto the second floor of a two-story walk-up building into an apartment that had a kitchen and living/dining area furnished with Formica and worn furniture. The walls were paper thin. Two twin beds squeezed into the single bedroom, across from a scarred dresser with an attached mirror and a shared closet. The bathroom peeked from behind the bedroom, completing the floor plan. No hallways, not one inch of extra space. A far cry from the cozy apartment on Strathmore Circle in Rochester where Mother and I once lived with my father and Smokey. The "garden" part of Raytown Gardens consisted of two massive trees and a little grass, barely enough for a bit of sunning on a summer day. But it felt good to be somewhere on our own, just Mother and me ... though I still missed Rochester, my home, our family. No doubt, my mother did as well.

Mother—still weakened, thin, and sometimes bleary-eyed—dragged herself to work. But over time, the shine crept back into her hair; the fog began to lift. Tentative smiles dimpled the corners of her eyes and tendrils of hope tickled at my heart.

Mother worked as a secretary in the front office of the Kansas City Athletics baseball franchise. I remember her in a skirt, a blouse, a wide belt encircling her narrow waist. All in matching lavender and lavender-and-white stripes. Chestnut tendrils framed her face as she applied makeup in

132

the morning. Still in bed, I followed her every move, admiring her beauty. With eyes scrunched shut, hoping she would think I was still asleep, I wondered—would the mother I remembered from New York come back to me one day?

Soon after she began working for the baseball team, a man appeared at our door ... right out of the blue. To Mother's smiling greeting, he strode in—wearing a suit and a tie and shoes of shiny black. His graying and gleamy hair slicked straight back from the sharp angles of his face. I suppose he saw himself as dapper. I gritted my teeth, the word "oily" coming to mind.

"Nancy, I would like you to meet Walt," Mother said. "Walt, this is my daughter, Nancy."

He smiled. I probably didn't. We exchanged stiff greetings.

"Walt works for the Athletics." Mother shot a nervous glance my way.

I unclenched my fists to accept the box of candies this unwelcome person thrust at me—delicacies from Kansas City's own Russell Stover—milky chocolates filled with fragrant soft orange crème. Clearly this visit had been planned in advance, without my knowledge.

I have no doubt I behaved badly. Rarely do children of a divorced mother embrace her first suitor with open arms, especially one who shows up by surprise. But, always with boxes of chocolates for me, Walt came again—and again.

Just as my mother had begun to come back to me, this man took her away. Mother announced that she and Walt

133

were going to spring training with the team. I was to stay with my best friend, Linda. That part was fine with me.

Linda had an older brother, a younger sister, a big jovial father and a tiny, sweet mother. They were a fun and caring family. Catholics, like me. I looked forward to times at Linda's house. She and I practiced cheers and fixed each other's hair. I put Linda's long blond hair up into a specially designed ponytail that only I knew how to create. I wanted one too, but my hair wasn't long enough to be fixed like that. And mine wasn't very blond anymore either.

Despite my envy at her hair, Linda felt like the sister I never had. She and I went to church together. Our new church was under construction so the masses were held in a temporary setting, a dance hall called the Chicken Coop. The Athletics baseball superstar, Roger Maris, attended our church. Furtive glimpses of the back of Roger Maris' head kept us returning week after week, despite the discomforts of sitting in cold metal folding chairs and the pain of kneeling on the hard, concrete floor. We looked like devout young Catholic girls, teenagers to be commended. I hoped no one guessed what I was really praying for—a chance to meet Roger Maris. Linda said she was offering her pain up to God. Clever girl—I wished I had thought of that.

After they returned from spring training, Walt came to see Mother more often. Sometimes he would show up on Saturday afternoons when Linda and I lay sunning ourselves on plastic woven lounge chairs in the tiny grassy area in front of the Raytown Gardens apartments.

"Watch out! Here he comes!"

Coated in baby oil and streaked with iodine, sweaty

and self-conscious in our two-piece bathing suits, we pretended to be asleep.

One night when I went to bed, Mother stayed up with Walt in the living room. I closed the flimsy bedroom door and fell asleep. That is, until strange loud sounds shook me awake. At the thumping and banging, I jumped out of bed, half asleep. Calling out, I threw open the bedroom door—into a darkened, steamy living room.

"Don't come in here! Close that door!" Mother's loud, harsh words jarred me. Time stood still and awareness dawned. My stomach lurched.

Abruptly slamming the door, I went back to bed, hating myself and both of them. I wished they hadn't come back from spring training. The pillow I stuffed around my head and ears didn't help me get to sleep. I don't know when Mother came to bed. We never spoke of the incident. I felt like I was the mother of a guilty teenager.

Mother and Walt dated a while longer. I looked at him with hooded eyes. Battle lines had been drawn; the chocolates stopped coming. But Walt was not the worst of the fates that lay ahead.

My mother was still in her thirties. With lustrous hair and deep brown eyes, she was good-looking . . . and, no doubt, lonely. But it didn't seem right that I should suffer the effects of my own mother's furtive and juvenile antics. Besides, as a typical teenager, I thought the social life in the family should be mine.

Inevitably, the next man came upon the scene. I convinced myself that I felt relief. It meant the end of Walt, the mom-robber, once and for all. Maybe this next guy wouldn't be so oily and sneaky.

At first, Calvin Smith was an improvement. He was well-known around Raytown—one of the sons of the Smith family, who owned Smith Brothers' Concrete. Their father was the mayor of Raytown. I didn't know it at first, but the sons had reputations . . . today they would be called bad boys. Wild ones.

I recall Calvin as a dusty character—faded blue jeans, scuffed work boots, brushy blond hair, muscular, tanned—not quite handsome, but someone who commanded a second glance. With his brusque manner and loud raspy voice, he reaped his share of attention. He took little notice of me. Every now and then he made me laugh, until such time as he wasn't funny anymore. When he moved into a brand-new duplex adjacent to the narrow railroad tracks which serviced the concrete store, Mother decided that we needed to move into the building right next door. I froze at this news.

In the fall of ninth grade, Linda and I and six other giddy girls had become cheerleaders. We displayed our silver monogrammed megaphone charms on long chains around our necks every day, with every outfit. Practices and games consumed our time and endless energies. We mastered the cheers and jumps. Sometimes Mother came to the football games. After watching us flit and flip about along the dusty sidelines, she pointed out that we should pay attention to what was going on in the game. Our cheers needed to support the action on the field. For instance, we shouldn't yell "Push 'em back, push 'em back, WAYYY back" when our team had the ball. My smart mother, once a cheerleader herself, took us under her wing. I beamed . . . and looked forward to cheering for basketball in the winter and then, next year, going to Raytown High School. There, at that venerable school on the stately hill overlooking our little junior high building, we would become RHS Bluejays . . . our dream.

"But, Mother," I said, when she told me we were moving, "those duplexes are south of 63rd Street. The kids from there have to go to the new school. Raytown South High School."

"Well, that won't happen to you," she said. "When we sign you up for high school, we'll tell the district you are living with Aunt Julie. You can live with me but we'll use Aunt Julie's address for you. She lives in the RHS area. You'll be able to go with your friends to Raytown High, I promise."

"I don't think that's how it works, Mother."

"Don't worry about it."

Despite my cries of protest, the discussion was over. She said she was sure the district would not find out. I was convinced they would, and I shook in fear and anger.

Though Mother argued that we needed a bigger place, I knew we were moving so she could live next to Calvin. I begged not to go. We moved anyway . . . taking Mother closer to Calvin, farther from me.

I opened the letter first. Through scalding tears, I read that I was assigned to Raytown South High School . . . the much-hated rival high school. Mother couldn't fix it. She took me to enroll. To be a Cardinal.

The new school was air-conditioned. The principal

led us into his frigid office. Mother tried to explain: she was divorced, I was an only child, all my friends were at RHS, I was an honor student, we had moved four times in the last four years, I wanted to stay at RHS and live with my aunt. The steely principal said he knew we had lied to avoid going to his school. He looked straight into my eyes. A chill snaked down my spine.

"I want you to know that you are off to a very poor start here. I do not expect that you will amount to much of anything at this school with this kind of beginning." Thus began my first year of high school.

Though he now lived in the next house, I did not see a lot of Calvin. When I did, he seemed big, loud and boisterous. Worrisome. Mother spent a lot of time at his place. No longer a cheerleader nor involved in many after-school activities, I spent a lot of time alone.

We met Rosie Cole, who lived in the other half of our duplex. Rosie was a good-looking divorcee with a handsome teenage son. Butch wore a blue and white letter jacket and was gone most of the time. I found out that since he was a senior—and the new high school did not yet have a senior class—Butch had been able to stay at Raytown High School, still a Bluejay. That hurt.

Mother and Rosie became friends. When they went out together after work, they came home late. I spent the time in my bedroom with my cherished pink Princess phone. The phone's cozy light glowed in the dark. I talked to friends and worked on school assignments. Even though I still felt out of place in the frosty halls of Raytown South High, I was determined that my grades would still be A's. I studied hard but pined for the warm corridors of RHS and for my Bluejay friends, connected now—not by shared experience—but by phone. The happy life I had envisioned on the northern side of 63rd Street was passing me by.

Midwestern weather in the summer and fall can be brutally hot. In late fall there came a typical steamy night. As usual, my bedroom window was open wide, curtains limp at each side. Heat and humidity filled the room. Despite the darkness outside, it was hard to sleep. My Princess phone's glow seemed to increase the temperature in the muggy bedroom. Only a thin window screen separated me from our darkened rear driveway and the deserted railroad tracks beyond that. Mother was next door, at Calvin's place. Again.

I lay in bed, sticky and half-asleep, when there came a sound outside my window . . . a twig snapping, a pebble scraping . . . something. My groggy eyes focused on that open window, that thin screen. Peering back at me was a shadowed face—a man's face—topped with a floppy hat. I froze . . . then leaped out of bed and stumbled into the kitchen. With shaking fingers, I dialed the wall phone.

At each unanswered ring, my heart beat harder. There came a hello.

Hushed and urgent, I said, "I need to talk to my mother!"

Mother came to the phone. "What's the matter, honey?"

"There's a man looking in my bedroom window! I was in bed and I saw his face through the screen! He has on a floppy hat like a hobo. I think he came off the tracks. Please come home now, Mom!" My teeth chattered despite the heat.

She did not answer right away. It sounded like she covered the phone and whispered something to Calvin. Why wasn't she racing to my side?

"There's no one out there, Nancy. Calvin is looking out the window and no one is over there. It must have been your imagination." Whispers of betrayal crept into my mind.

"I saw him, Mom. I heard something, too. I'm sure I did."

"It was just your imagination, Nancy, or maybe a dream. You don't need to worry. I'm right next door, and there's nobody over there. Go back to your room and close the window. Pull the curtains closed, too. I'll be home later on."

"But I'm scared, Mom. And it's hot in there. I won't be able to go to sleep. Please come home."

"There's nothing to be afraid of. Really. Take the fan from my bedroom and turn it on. You don't need me there. I'm right next door. I'll be home later." Her words chilled me more than the hobo's shadow. When I forced myself back to bed, his shadow was gone. But her answers lived on.

Mother did not come home then, and I didn't see her when she did. But I didn't forget what I had seen, how I felt, what I heard my mother say. I remember it all . . . from the glow of the Princess phone to the floppy hat to the muffled sound of Mother's voice over the phone. And when that connection broke, I felt a splintering in my heart. I never forgot that night.

Mostly it was miserable in that duplex beside the railroad tracks, beside Calvin Smith. But sometimes Rosie would invite Mother and me to her cabin at the Lake of the Ozarks. There, the twinkling lake would wink us awake in the mornings. In Rosie's moldy little boat, we would glide over diamond ripples in the afternoons. The waters turned to molten gold at sunset. Although the aged wooden cabin smelled musty, and sometimes we would spot a mouse or two, I felt a magic on the banks of that lovely lake, beside those lapping waters. In the quiet cove, floating on a solitary rubber raft beneath wispy clouds, amid whispering waves, I imagined a world without Calvin Smith—a world in which I was still a Bluejay. But the idyllic weekends always came to an end, and I would find myself right back next door to him. A reluctant Cardinal once again.

Sometimes when Mother came home after a night with Calvin, she would be sniffling. At times I saw blood on the tissues. Other times she went straight to her bedroom. Days later, I would notice bruises on her arms or neck. We didn't talk about them. We didn't talk much in those days, like two leery juveniles circling one another.

But then there was a night when Mother returned to our duplex very late, calling to me with an unnerving screech. I found her crumpled on the couch, holding her wrist and bleeding from her nose. Like a grown-up would do, I grabbed a cloth and ice.

She told me to get in the car. Somehow, since I could not, she managed to drive . . . to a fancy house on Blue Ridge Boulevard. I knew the place. The mayor lived there. Mayor Smith, Calvin's father. Mother demanded that I go up to the

141

porch with her.

"You have to help me."

"No, Mother. We can't go up there. It's the middle of the night. We need to go to the hospital." Through my fear and dread, I struggled to change her mind.

She would not be deterred. Horrified, I helped her onto the wide porch where she rang the doorbell time and again. After what seemed like forever, old Mr. Smith cracked open the door. His huge naked belly protruded as he fumbled for the belt of a red plaid bathrobe. He was not wearing underwear. His eyes flashed; mine dropped to the ground. In a voice filled with thunder he roared, "Violet. What the hell are you doing here? It's the middle of the night."

With ice to nose and left wrist askew, Mother strained to stand up straight. I cowered behind her—a terrified fourteen-year-old, dying inside.

"Can you see what he did? Do you see what your son did to me? Look at me! You have to look at me!"

To my ears, Mother's demands sounded like those of a frightened but petulant child. There must have been more to that surreal exchange, but there was no sympathy, no resolution. We were not invited in.

Somehow, we made it to the hospital where I assisted my staggering mother into the emergency room. I waited a long time for her broken nose and wrist to be treated. And I thought of another night on which others had supported her sagging figure around and around a tiny front yard.

Mother's injuries were not the only things fixed on that dreadful night. Fixed also were bitter memories . . .

cemented forever in my mind. Memories of a living nightmare, one in which I had to grow up overnight.

Mother's wounds healed. The physical ones, at least. Broken bones knitted; scars formed. For me, it was not bones but a supporting bough that had broken. And my cradle, which had begun its descent on a frosty night under a gleaming full moon four years prior, fell—once and for all. In that instant, in mind and soul, my bond to my mother snapped. A crusty cast encased me like the shell of a turtle. I retracted and quivered, afraid to peek beyond my carapace, to risk being crushed again by my mother . . . a mother now looming outside the reaches of my hardening heart.

Calvin moved, right away. I didn't find out where he went and I didn't care. Mother and I stayed in the duplex a while longer, me living in fear that the story of that dreadful event would spread like wildfire throughout the community. But my school responsibilities diverted me and I managed to end the year with straight A's, getting elected to be Vice-President of the Pep Squad and into the National Honor Society. At the Induction, the principal came over.

"I guess I was wrong about you," he said, with a sheepish grin.

And I said goodbye. "We're moving again. I'll be going back to Raytown High next year."

Mother had met yet another man.

A Red Convertible

*F*or pioneers of the mid-1800s, it was the first stop on the Santa Fe Trail—the blacksmith shop of William Ray, after whom Raytown was later named—a scant eight miles south of those settlers' brave start in nearby Independence, Missouri. In later years we joked that Raytown's founders were the pioneer quitters.

The spot upon which William Ray's shop arose became the intersection of Blue Ridge Boulevard and Raytown Road—the center of that little town, my world. In the 1960s, at that very junction, sat an iconic little pharmacy. Behind the prescription counter of Muir Drugs worked Fred Armstrong, the friendly pharmacist with a salt-and-pepper flat-top. Fred was well-known among the citizens of Raytown, having advised upon and dispensed their ointments, preparations, remedies, and medications for years. His pharmacy station flanked the soda fountain, a favorite watering hole for the teenage students of Raytown High School who stopped in for sodas and treats on their walks home from school. When there was a lull in his primary duties, Fred would lend a hand behind the soda counter. He bantered with the students, delivering corny jokes and dorky little quips. The kids smiled and laughed with Fred even while snickering and rolling their eyes behind his back. He was an over-the-hill mascot to those juvenile self-anointed sophisticates of the little blue-collar town. Fred's fun-loving greetings and silly grins enlivened their homework-laden afternoons.

There were occasional sightings of Fred tooling around town in his red Cadillac convertible . . . an eye-catching vehicle with huge pointy fins and snappy, white-walled tires. While it seemed unusual that a goofy guy like Fred would drive something like that, a playboy's car, we loved seeing him go by. The students, especially the boys, salivated at the thought of a ride in that tantalizing set of wheels. That's how the youth of Raytown, myself included, came to know Fred Armstrong.

After a time, though I know not how, my mother found her way into that exotic convertible. Zipping about town with Fred, she looked like a movie star—long dark tresses blowing in the wind, scarf around her neck, big sunglasses. No longer, I knew with relief, were there ugly cuts and bruises behind those oversized shades. Her hard-fisted "friend" Calvin was out of the picture . . . for me, not soon enough.

I began to wonder, in the manner of an only child adept at envisioning fantasies for herself: what if Mother and Fred became a couple? In response to Fred's quirky disposition, Mother's laugh, long in hibernation, had reemerged. And the best thing was that Fred made me laugh, too. I imagined what a great stepfather he would be. He seemed to want to be a part of my life as much as he wanted to be with Mother. This turned out to be true.

Mother and I, sometimes accompanied by my friends, loved riding around Raytown with Fred in his snazzy convertible. We waved at everyone and many waved back. He was a Man-About-Town, the friendly, funny pharmacist. Did Mother have her sights set on Fred? My fantasies richened.

I can't say how it all came about. At the time, I was fifteen. As Fred became a regular around us, I had loosened up. My persona as a typical teenager — one of those famously egocentric beings with the mercurial moods — began to emerge. I quipped, laughed, and sparred at home. My mother unfurled like the tentative petals of a new blossom. A blooming Violet. I think we both began to trust life a bit, and I felt relieved of my obligation to be my mother's keeper.

And then Mother told me she was pregnant.

Well, then. How did I feel about that? I had wished for a sister or brother my whole life. I was crazy about Fred. Mother was healthy again, happier than I could remember. But she was not married. In fact, she was divorced. And now pregnant. Such an unexpected wrinkle in the typical mother/daughter scenario. Wasn't I the one who should have been thinking about pregnancy, and how I would negotiate the coming years without getting into trouble?

That's what my cousin told me, though eventually it turned out that she herself was not so smart about those matters. This new development was as humiliating as it was happy . . . a pregnant, unwed mother. I feared telling anyone. And yet, my heart leapt.

Mother and Fred went away for a weekend to Miami, Oklahoma, where they could get married without delay. Their "quickie" marriage had my blessing, for sure. And, as luck would have it, one of my school friends' mothers turned out to be pregnant, too. That mom was married, but nevertheless. Now I wasn't the only fifteen-year-old in Raytown with a pregnant mother. It was all good, for a while. Quite a while, until it wasn't.

Mother and I had moved away from the hated railroad tracks and our troublesome neighbor. Back to my beloved school district and my old friends, Linda and others, who convinced the benevolent drill-team sponsor into letting me onto the team. There was one stipulation, however, since I hadn't been there the previous spring for official tryouts. She announced that the drill team needed a drummer and, luckily, I had come along. So I promised to learn to play a drum, and fast. AND to play it while marching. I took drum lessons, bought that little inclined rubber practice pad and some drumsticks, and I tried. I really did. But I hadn't had any training on a musical instrument since floundering with the flute and clarinet in third grade. I couldn't read music, much less play a drum and march at the same time. Though my career as a drummer never worked out, I got to stay on the drill team anyway. I was ever grateful to my friends, our sponsor and my lucky stars.

I also had a new baby sister. Little Alison was a dark-haired, dark-eyed beauty like my mother ... my lifetime hope for a sibling, come true. Not the age-mate companion I had long prayed for, perhaps, but a precious little one who brightened our days. We laughed when Alison—not yet potty trained—pooped on the fireplace hearth and said, "Inky did it."

A home, a family, a sister, my favorite school, friends, sweet Inky dog. My mother. A father. Finally, a father. It was like living a dream.

Our little two-bedroom, A-frame rental home sat across the street from Kemp's Lake. There were crawdads to catch in the summer. The little lake froze in the winter—we would ice skate over the bumps on its wind-tossed hardened surface. Our backyard proved to be a perfect place to practice marching, drills, acrobatics and cheers. In the little living room with the beamed ceiling and skylights, I played a brand-new album with jaunty tunes of an outrageous British singing sensation, the Beatles—time and time again. There were rousing Scrabble games. My parents tried to teach me to play bridge ... a nightmare for me and them, but otherwise my dreams were good.

A much-anticipated day arrived ... the day to pick up senior class rings at the jewelry store across the street from Muir Drugs. We were officially seniors—the class of RHS '65. I had earned my driver's license. That evening, Mother let me drive her car. A few friends and I piled into that green Chevy Bel Air with the menacing stick shift. Well tutored by Fred, I shifted smoothly and proudly. That night, our group—upstanding girls, fully involved, good students—drove to the woodsy roads of the nearby countryside, looking for unadorned railroad bridges and overpasses. We had secreted away some cans of spray paint to adorn these structures with "RHS '65" in the grand tradition of newly anointed senior class members. As I drove along, though, out of my element, I found myself gripping the wheel with white knuckles and suppressing my relief when we didn't find anything to paint along those dark, deserted roads. We began to retell stories of one-armed snaggle-toothed hobos who were said to have jumped out upon unsuspecting illicit couples in their fogged-up cars parked deep within the blackened woods. Subdued and shaky, though buoyed by our shiny new senior rings, we headed home, and I don't think I was the only one who started to breathe again.

I had dropped everyone off except one last cohort in crime, my nearby neighbor. We headed up Raytown Road, which was deserted of traffic at that hour. The blank white cement-block side of a now shuttered-up former dairy building came into view, practically begging us to anoint it with an RHS '65 logo.

Almost in unison, we said, "It's perfect!"

I parked in a shadow and we hopped from the car. Spraying with giddy abandon, with not a single unbidden headlight to interrupt us, we worked in a breathless frenzy. But we didn't count on the building's owner living right next door. Nor on him spying us—with fury in his eyes.

"Quick! Get in!" I said.

We sprang into our car . . . and he into his. The

ensuing high-speed chase through the narrow backroads of Raytown was a challenge for me and that gear shift, especially while racing to cross the railroad tracks with a train in sight, but I managed to stay ahead of both the train and our determined pursuer until he ran us off the road in front of the Raytown Police Department.

"Get out! You're going in!" he said, purple-faced. "You ruined my building and you are going to pay for this, you unruly hoodlums!"

Hoodlums? I had done only one other thing wrong in all my years in school—my kindergarten fiasco. Granted, I got caught for that too, but really? Characteristically, I began to cry. And sob. My wide-eyed accomplice froze. With her huge brown eyes, she looked shell-shocked.

"Oh, no. Please, mister. We're not hoodlums. Please just follow me home. Talk to my father. I live really close and I'll go really slow the whole way. Please just follow me home."

That good Raytowner relented. He did as I asked . . . followed me as I drove at no more than five miles an hour until skidding up the loose gravel driveway of our little house across from Kemp's Lake. Sobbing and crying, I raced into the house.

"Fred, Fred . . . come quick! Help!" Thank heaven, he was home. I gasped the story to him as we went through the carport and out to face the music. Our irate pursuer had made his way up the darkened driveway. We could just make out his image. Both men stopped short.

With the hint of a grin, Fred said, "Well, hello, Bob . . . that's you, isn't it?"

"Fred ... Fred Armstrong! Well, well. Imagine our meeting up like this!" A tiny smile teased the corners of his mouth. "I hate to tell you this, but there's some trouble. Your girl. This problem child here."

With arms around each other's shoulders, Fred and Bob made amends—and plans.

My brown-eyed buddy and I had to pay for the white paint ourselves. We didn't expect an audience for the repainting event on Saturday morning—we even left the rollers in our hair—but there was a small crowd ... other classmates, a few parents. Some pictures of the spectacle made their way into the RHS '65 yearbook. But after we finished, the building looked shiny and new again. Fred had saved the day.

Our expanded family needed a bigger home. We moved just around the corner onto Elm Street, into a handsome ranch house with weathered gray shingles and two bedrooms upstairs. I got my own spacious bedroom in the basement with a bathroom all to myself. An outside door led right into the carport. I didn't start sneaking out that door until a few years later, when I was home from college. There was also a downstairs family room with a fireplace. Dear Inky had passed, but we got a black miniature poodle and named him Lancelot. Despite having our own Lancelot, Fred was my knight in shining armor. By his very presence, he showed me that there could be joy in life, that love is better than hate. And he taught me to laugh at myself. When I would make a typical juvenile statement, he would say, "How can somebody so smart be so stupid?" Always with a twinkle in his eye.

Fred also tried to teach me to not sweat the small stuff. When I shared my teenage traumas, depending upon the severity, he sometimes would say, "In ten years, Nancy, is this really going to make any difference?" The question infuriated me. A teenager lives in the present, not ten years out. Sometimes Fred was right, but sometimes he wasn't. After ten years, plenty of things still made a difference.

High school graduation came and went amid typical bittersweet smiles and tears. Only a handful of classmates had applied to the University of Missouri, 250 miles away in Columbia, and I was one of them. We celebrated my acceptance, and that of my steady boyfriend, John. But there were trepidations in the family. Arguments. Worries about money. I had scholarships, loans and a summer job, but college was going to be a financial drain, and I knew it.

I sent a letter to my father in New York, telling him that my mother had a job and worked hard, but she didn't make a lot of money. It was probably a mistake to mention that Mother and Fred were raising another young daughter. I received a card from my father. He sent a twenty-five-dollar check for my eighteenth birthday and explained that he didn't care one bit about my sister and wouldn't be contributing to my college education. He did, however, congratulate me on my acceptance to the University.

No one on Mother's side of the family had gone to college. But now there was Fred, with his degree and invaluable insights earned on a GI bill from the University of Chicago. That summer, he and I engaged in deep discussions and heated debates, often raging until the wee hours of the morning. We examined books and politics and college life. We laughed at silly jokes. We talked about everything.

It was 1965, and there were storm clouds brewing throughout the country. But, sequestered in a small, insular midwestern town—and bubbled within the self-absorption of teenagerhood—I knew little of that. My prayers were for red Capezio shoes, not justice and world peace. Fred asked if I knew there would be Jewish people and black students at my college, perhaps even in my dormitory, or assigned as my roommate.

"It will be good for you to get to know a variety of people," he said. Having grown up in the homogeneous community of Raytown, I needed to know how to do that . . . to honor both similarities and differences. My wise stepfather shared his many experiences and advice.

Unlike most everyone else in the family, I did not smoke or drink alcohol. My girlfriends and I barely spoke to girls who did those things. The boys in our class were another matter, but, of course, they were the boys. We liked them and thus overlooked their transgressions.

Fred made a prediction. "Within six months at college, you will be smoking and drinking."

"I will not. Never. You're wrong." We agreed on a bet.

The bet turned out to be a draw. It took less than six months . . . less than six weeks . . . for me to develop a taste for Boone's Farm Apple Wine at John's fraternity parties on the steep rocky cliffs above the muddy Missouri River. But Fred lost the part about the smoking.

So there I was, away at college, heady with freedom

154

and newfound challenges. Fred, Mother and Alison were back in Raytown—with storm clouds looming about them. I knew of their fighting and the heavy drinking . . . increasing every year. (It would be a long time before I learned about the drugs). On holidays and summers at home, my basement bedroom was no longer a safe haven. It became the place that Mother and Fred stalked in the middle of the night. They descended on me to referee their arguments—loud verbal battles which confounded me. Quarrels about money, loyalties . . . disputes about anything and everything. Walking a tightrope to remain neutral, I infuriated them both, adding fuel to their fires. I prayed that Alison, in her little bedroom upstairs, could not hear the madness. Later I learned that when I moved away, Alison became their referee, as early as age seven.

Clearly, a dark funnel was forming . . . but I immersed myself in demanding college studies, my summer jobs, my friends, and John—my now-fiancée—and, by 1968, our happy wedding plans. As if wearing blinders, I ignored—denied—the brewing storm at home. But the seeds of destruction were sown. They would germinate for over ten years. For more than a decade, the upheaval rose, piece by excruciating piece.

When the storm finally broke, bitter swirling winds overcame Mother and Fred, who spun in opposite directions. The angry twister overwhelmed Alison as well. Always having been closer to her dad, she spurned Mother, our aunt and cousins. The entire family landscape exploded. As a Midwesterner, I had weathered tornados and their effects. The aftermath of this family storm would prove to be the most destructive of all.

I was an adult when Fred went away, and my heart broke. He had saved me as a teenager, been my confidante and debate partner during the college years. He had fathered, and nurtured, my precious little sister . . . walked me down the aisle at my wedding . . . been a grandfather to my sons. He was a lifeline. And then he was gone, out of my life. Another father whisked away. I hurt as deeply as I had at age ten — when Kermit walked out — reeling at yet another loss of a father, this time a sibling, a family.

Though the wounds ached, a fuming anger boiled up within me. How could this cycle be repeating itself once again? Weren't we all adults, beyond this kind of chaos? Couldn't everyone just grow up and live out their lives in a semblance of harmony or, at the very least, civilized behavior? I was furious with every one of them, and saddened for myself, my husband and our sons.

By this time, 1978, John and I had moved to Pennsylvania with the boys, ages six months and four years. Busy establishing our careers and committed to maintaining firm, stable ground under the boys' feet, we had little energy for additional drama. It seemed clear that Aunt Julie would be Mother's main support system in Kansas City. I faced a drastic choice. In truth, I longed for Fred and Alison to remain a part of my life and the lives of my sons. Yet I knew Mother and Aunt Julie were both insane with bitterness toward Fred, and Alison, whom they viewed as an unforgivably disloyal daughter. If I was going to have a mother in my life, a grandmother for my sons, I had to choose them. And though it was as painful as amputating a limb, I cut off all contact with Fred and Alison. I could not know then that Mother's fate—spawned in that wicked storm back in the Midwest—was already sealed, regardless.

Our perceptive, mature-beyond-his-age firstborn son was in college when he asked, "Mom, would it be okay with you if I contacted Fred?"

Stifling a sob, I answered, "Absolutely. It makes me so happy that you want to do that. Please get in touch." I had never wanted the skeletons in my closet to be a part of my children's lives.

Fred was a changed and sober man . . . living a happy life in nearby Paola, Kansas, with a loving wife, still working as a pharmacist. He had missed us. With typical generosity of spirit, he told me he understood why we had divorced ourselves from him. We began to have regular visits filled with sentimental reminiscences and debates for old time's sake. In time, he attended the graduations and weddings of both our boys. Happily, our connections to Alison rekindled as well. Once again, she was dear "Auntie" to her beloved nephews.

Over time, Fred's health declined. With each year, there came a new concern. One day, I wrote him a letter.

Dear Fred,

Alison wrote that you are having your other stent put in on Monday and it sounds like the procedure might be a difficult one. I want you to know how much you are, and have been, in my thoughts and prayers.

As the years go by, with loved ones facing the inevitable difficult times that come along, I find myself reflecting and wanting to share important thoughts that, for one reason or another, have remained unshared. Such is the case with you. A gap of fourteen years is difficult to fill, but I'd like to try.

I owe you a great debt of gratitude for many things. You should know that as I reflect upon my life, I recognize that had you not appeared at the times that you did, I could never have developed the foundation to become the person I am today. For me, you were the anchor upon which that foundation grew. As rocky as times sometimes were, you brought to my teenage years a sense of love and fun and family that I desperately needed. I have always been grateful for that.

Even more importantly in my estimation, because of you and you alone, my sons know the meaning of the word "grandfather." They treasure their memories of their early years with you and care deeply about you. How fitting it is that one of them bridged for us that gap of fourteen years and opened the door to recently shared times that are precious memories to me and to them.

I will always be saddened that I allowed my complicated connections to my mother to get in the way of a relationship with you. Having felt strongly that I disappointed Mother during her lifetime, I found I could not handle a relationship that, to me, seemed a further betrayal of her in death. In doing this, I robbed my boys, and myself, of our connection with you for far too long. It is a regret that I will always feel . . . time too precious to have been lost. How wonderful it was, however, that once the door was opened, you came back into our lives graciously, meaningfully, and without judgment. To have had you at the boys' graduations is a gift that we all treasure. And last year's ski trip provided a healing for me that was long overdue. Thank you for giving me time to get beyond the ghosts of my past, and for not holding them against me.

I can still hear you say, during the numerous great and small crises of my teenage years, that in ten years I wouldn't even remember the current crisis du jour. As furious as that made me, in some instances, you were right. But there are plenty of crises that I DO remember . . . those which shaped who I am and where my life has gone . . . and in my remembrances, you are always there, always listening, never judging . . . helping me to know when to burn and when to rebuild bridges, and to recognize those instances in which the necessity was merely to repaint the building.

Just as I did on an August day in 1968 walking down the aisle at St. Bernadette's Church, I will always feel that you were the closest thing to a "real" father I ever had, and you cannot know how grateful I am to you for that . . . and for being a grand grandfather to our sons, the only grandfather with whom they have ever truly bonded. Thank you, Fred.

We look forward to many special times with you in the future. Our hearts and hopes will be with you on Monday; our gratitude and love are with you always . . . Nancy

Our time with Fred did not end that year. We continued to enjoy treasured connections and good times together. But the inevitable day came seven years later, when Fred lost his battle with health and age. His last words to me, said with a deep sigh, were, "I'm going home." I detected relief in his utterance.

To this day — in my dreams — I have been known to ride in a snappy red convertible with wide, shiny fins . . . to glide through the sky with a dorky, flat-topped, grinning wise guy at the wheel. And when I wake up, I smile.

Tough Love

*P*ittsburgh, Pennsylvania, September 1985. I sit in an improvised office in a book storage closet on the second floor of the high school building, the first private office I've ever had. Last month, I was a special education classroom teacher, looking for a professional change . . . somewhere to apply the principles from my newly earned Certificate in Educational Leadership. Today, I am the Elementary Gifted Program Coordinator for the school district, planning a teacher in-service workshop, to take place in just over a month. Despite the sparse surroundings, my recharged brain overflows with ideas and anticipation for my new position. But I have yet to learn what else the month has in store.

Though ecstatic at having secured this coveted job, my heart is heavy. In Kansas City, my mother has been in critical condition. Her stomach was pumped. Revived and alive, she was admitted to a psychiatric treatment center, where I left a message with the doctor.

The phone rings. It is Mother's psychiatrist.

"Hello, Doctor," I say. "Thank you for returning my call."

I say a silent prayer of thanks at the timing. Secreted away in my 'office,' the book storage closet, I am free to speak.

"Yes, Nancy. We need to talk, but I don't have a long time today."

He clears his throat. "Your mother is going to recover, physically at least. Her emotional issues are the challenge. I want you to be aware of our plan."

I weigh my words. "It's nothing new, as I'm sure you know. She's tried to take her life many times. I'm sure my aunt has filled you in."

"Yes, she has. But I'd like to hear from you."

Again, I select my words carefully. "Aunt Julie and Gretchen have taken care of mother's overdoses many times. It started when I was ten and my father left. Maybe before that, I don't know. Now that Fred and Alison have left, the cycle is repeating. Getting worse."

"Your mother's issues must have affected you."

"Yes, they did. For years. Especially from age ten until she remarried. It was like I was raising her and not the other way around."

"Are you close to your mother?"

"We were never close. I grew up feeling insecure, untrusting. When I most needed her, in my early teens, she wasn't there for me. Now I hold her at arm's length."

"Why?"

"For my survival. With Mother, with the whole family, everybody knows everything. It's not the way I want to live. I don't want them to be involved in my private life. It doesn't work. They're too dramatic, controlling. There's too much chaos. It's not healthy."

I take a breath.

"And I don't think I can do anything for my mother, anyway . . . short of bringing her here and letting her live with us."

"Have you considered that?"

"Never."

He asks how my family in Pittsburgh would be affected if I were to move Mother there.

"It would tear us apart. I can't and won't do that to my husband, my marriage, myself."

The next words are a knife to my heart, but I continue.

"I know my mother wants to move here with us. To be taken care of since Fred and Alison are gone. She is furious with me that we won't rescue her. The last time we talked, before this latest overdose, she told me that I haven't ever helped her." I pause. The doctor is silent.

"But we can't bring her here. It wouldn't fix her. Nothing ever has. Our boundaries would make her miserable. My greatest fear is that she would end up getting upset and trying to take her life again . . . with my sons around and aware." I swallow.

With bated breath, I venture to ask, "Do you think it would be good to bring her here?"

"It would be the worst thing you could do, for

everyone."

I breathe again. Finally, validation.

He says, "I'm sure you've heard of enabling."

"I think that's what the family has been doing for a long time. Aunt Julie and Gretchen have housed her, fed her, tolerated her self-destruction. They've treated her breakdowns and overdoses. And before them, my grandparents and I did the same things."

"This has enabled your mother . . . to be weak and unwell. To remain dependent upon others," he says. "Your mother needs to stand on her own if she's ever going to get better. Are you familiar with 'tough love'?"

"I know about tough love. But it's never been that kind of family. Everyone is always bailing everyone else out, taking them in, patching them up. My mother isn't the only one. It's how they are."

"Tell me about that."

I soften my tone. "They're not a tough-love type family. They 'adopt' people, Mother and others . . . prop them up, rescue them, take on their problems and then take over. The old-school, extended family approach, I guess. They're a forceful, take-charge family with open arms for all. Only the ones who cut the cord, moved away, have successful marriages . . . myself, my sister Alison, my cousin Gary. Gretchen left but came back. She got wrapped up in the whole dynamic again. I think it has cost her a lot."

"There's much to discuss, but we don't have the time now. What I will say is that your aunt and cousin, in their minds, are acting out of love. But it's also control, which—in a way—is what they know. They mean well, but this hasn't helped your mother. You recognize the problem. Although it's late, she has to learn to swim, or she'll continue to sink. I'll work to help your family deal with that. It's not impossible."

"I hope you can. I've never understood how to get Mother to want to be independent. I tried as a teenager and afterward, but it was never enough. She can't handle not having a man in her life, I know. But when she was at her best, she had a job. She was always good at her jobs. Confident. I've talked to her about that, tried to encourage her to go to work now—even just part time—for her own good. But she says she's too sick."

"Your mother is a casualty of a lifetime of dependence. And you are right . . . if she's ever going to get well, she must be independent. That will be the message from us here at the clinic, with her and all the family. And the focus of our therapy—to teach her to stand on her own two feet. She needs to know that others can't bail her out anymore. This is a difficult concept for a fragile sixty-year-old. We have our work cut out."

"I'll do whatever I can to help."

I hear a deep breath. "You should all prepare yourselves. She may not survive."

My heart skips a beat. The hair on my neck rises as though there is a sudden draft, colder than my mother's last words to me. I sense the statement is literal.

He gives the same message to my aunt, uncle, and cousin. Exhausted, they agree. We talk about it. I think they have finally seen they can't save my mother. I wonder if anyone can.

DON'T FAULT THE MOON

Mother does well at the clinic. A savvy patient, she knows what to say and do. In just three weeks, she is released. She moves back to Aunt Julie's house. No one realizes she has a plan.

Mother calls and tells me she is out of money and needs twelve-hundred dollars to pay her bills. I have many questions but ask few. I say I am glad she is out of the hospital. Tell her she sounds good. Venture to ask if she is thinking about looking for a job. It's a frosty exchange.

"No, I'm not." Her voice is sharp as a knife. "The first thing I need to do is pay these bills, and I need you to send me the money."

All part of her plan. I should have asked my questions.

We can help; my husband agrees. I can't say no, despite the warning bell about "enabling." We send Mother a check, unknowingly facilitating her plan.

The call comes at dinnertime. I answer on the third ring. The next words, from Kansas City, alter the world.

Aunt Julie is on the line. Her abrupt message washes over me like a frigid wave. My eyes close; a tortured breath escapes my lips. With heart pounding louder than my voice, I turn to my husband and say, "It's over."

He holds me tight as I crumple to my knees.

My cousin Gary calls from Hawaii. He quotes the Rolling Stones — something about not getting what you want but getting what you need. I think he means Mother, but I'm not sure.

We pack for the funeral. I am numb from Pittsburgh to Kansas City. From Kansas City back home. A lifetime in four days.

Back at work, I conduct my first in-service program, just days following the funeral. The teachers stand to applaud; they have heard of Mother's death. With brimming eyes, I give silent thanks for my colleagues and this job. Work is my salvation.

Mother's plan unfolds. The modest estate is settled. It turns out that a bill we covered was her life insurance premium. It provides for each of our sons, her grandsons, a small inheritance ... the sum total of her net worth, in dollars and cents, on this Earth.

Her true value, her legacy, is yet to be calculated.

Message to a Mother

*I*t was not my idea to write this letter. I wrote it in 2009, at age sixty-two.

To my mother: V. M. R. H. A.

I hope you are in Heaven. For whatever reasons, I believe that your life on Earth was mostly a living Hell. I've felt guilty every day of my life for that. I knew some of your story. But now the time has come for you to know mine.

You were my mother and, as the country song says, because of you, I am afraid. Maybe the only time I ever knew true safety and security in my life was when I was in the womb. But most certainly it ended when this ten-year-old was awakened in the middle of the night by her mother saying goodbye. That she loved her, but that she wouldn't be there in the morning because she had taken a bottle of sleeping pills. You left it up to your ten-year-old daughter to wake the rest of the house to save you? Did you envision that the image and sensation of walking you barefoot in circles on the frozen grass of the front yard would be seared into the consciousness of that child for the rest of her life? Were you aware that, until that daughter left home for college, she never said goodnight to you without saying, "See you in the morning?" And if you didn't say it back, she stayed up until you did? This is the fear that has defined my life, and I live with it still. Not a day goes by in which I don't fear that my world might come crashing down around me. I am fifty-two years old, and because of you, I am afraid.

For a while, once my active memory began, at maybe five or six years, I was a child. We had a home. No brothers or sisters, but I had a cat and then a beloved dog. I loved school and my friends. My father built an ice-skating rink in the back yard. We went on vacation. I rode my bike to school and my mother was in the PTA. We went to church and I was a Brownie Scout. I jumped on a pogo stick. It was good, and then it was gone.

He left and we had to go, and after that, it was all about you. Pills and treatments and hospitals and doctors. No home, no money, tears and anger. You couldn't care for me and he didn't want me, and I was always the extra baggage that nobody seemed to know what to do with. We lived with whoever we could and I went from school to school. It was always school that saved me in those days. In school I was safe and normal and good. I did well. I never wanted to leave. I became a teacher.

I am afraid, and I am guilty, and I want to feel love for you, but I can only feel anger, sometimes hate. And then I feel worse . . . more guilt . . . more hatred, for myself.

I tried to save you for a while, but then I quit . . .

There are many nights, to this day, that I don't go to sleep at all . . .

Late in his life, I asked my father to tell me about you when the two of you were young. I guess I waited too long. He didn't have much to say. It has just begun to dawn on me that having me was probably the worst thing that happened to him, and to you, too. As much as I begged, there were no more children. Neither of you knew what to do with a child. It seems you didn't have a clue what to do with a marriage, or what to do with anything outside of yourselves. You both said you loved me, but in reality what you did was leave.

I don't think you had energy or stamina to give to anything outside of yourself. My father told me that my childhood in New York ended because you couldn't be happy there, couldn't live without your parents. I couldn't have a father in part because you couldn't live without yours. And I get to be the guilty one? Go figure.

Fortunately, you married Fred and I loved him, and Alison when she came. There were some happy times before the drinking and the fighting and the drugs began.

It was probably because of you that I had little confidence as a mother. Was your sabotage purposeful? And yet, I have two incredibly wonderful and successful sons. Would that make you happy or jealous?

There are good things I remember:
Easter baskets in Rochester
My First Communion
You polishing John's shoes for the high school football games
Your love for your grandsons
But . . . when I think of my mother over the years, I think sad. You were sad living in Rochester. You were sad at my

wedding. You were always sad. Shrinking Violet. You never wanted to be where you were, unless it was with your own mother. You cried a lot, a curse you passed to me. I cannot ever remember a time of joy in your life. Anxiety, sadness, depression, fear. Your nemeses . . . the things I now fight. Does this make you, finally, happy?

In our last conversation, I told you that you were going to have to save yourself. For the sake of myself and my own family, I said, I had to stop trying to save you. You told me I never had.

Can you comprehend the hole in the heart of a person who is robbed of love for her mother? That would be me. I know I loved you once, but at a point that love turned to resentment and more. Perhaps the turning point was when my childhood disappeared and I became the mother. Maybe you lived years of torture with the knowledge of what that night with your ten-year-old really meant. You were right. In reality, that night never ended. I don't know if it ever will. And I am afraid.

Mother had been gone twenty-four years before I sought the help of a therapist. My stoic persona regarding all matters about my mother had frayed. For various reasons, ghosts of the past haunted my present. Buried mistrust, fear, and insecurity—all too much on my mind. I decided I needed help.

I might have pulled every tooth in my mouth, one by one, and found more pleasure, less pain, than in those hated therapy sessions. I shocked myself at the rawness of my emotions, the depth of my anger, after all those years. The therapist said there had been no closure. She told me to write a letter to my mother, so I did. The letter didn't help. Quite the contrary. I needed to close Pandora's box again. Unable to bear the gut-wrenching sessions any longer, convinced I would figure things out on my own, I wrapped the meetings up — together with my raw emotions and hot tears. Amid misty sighs of relief, I returned my focus to family, job, friends . . . my healing salve.

This time, the wounds closed, the scabs shrunk, my scars faded. Like broken bones after time, my framework knitted — stronger than before. And with healing grew a guarded acceptance.

For years, I felt life had dealt me a raw deal — an uncaring father, a damaged mother, a fractured family, a disjointed existence. But life, and luck, prevailed . . . I persevered, achieved, and married an impossibly good man. We had beautiful children. That husband, beyond competent as a father, shouldered with me the critical work of parenting.

I admitted to myself that my mother had almost no support. I came to see the odds she had faced as fearsome, astounding. And that . . . from her, others, and painful experiences . . . I inherited strength.

Did Violet fail as a mother? Absolutely.

Did I fail as her daughter? Without a doubt.

Were we able to bolster one another? Rarely.

Was it all inevitable? Maybe.

Such was our shared tragedy . . . the story of that mother and this daughter.

Last Words

*C*ould you write a dialogue for the final words you would exchange with a loved one? Or rewrite a drama that had already been performed? Would you want to, if you could?

Permit me, if you will, one flight of fantasy. Today's scenario does not occur in a frigid gray airport waiting area. Nor is it a last bristling, bitter telephone call. This musing is neither of those realities but, rather, a foray into fiction. Let's see how far we get.

Imagine a hearth-warmed, golden room smelling of wood smoke, home cooking and the possibility of tenderness. Diffuse, flickering light softening two furrowed brows. Mother and daughter seated in overstuffed comfy corduroy chairs; even so, facing one another with a certain stiffness. At their sides, tawny drinks, steaming in tall, curvy glass mugs, wafting scents of citrus and herb. It is not a place either has seen before, nor will they see it again. It is a good

175

place for a different dialogue. *Would it be?*

A stilted start. "We should get on with this. Nancy. We don't have a lot of time."

Softly, "I know. Mother. Let's do the best we can."

From beneath veiled eyes come Mother's throaty words. "What do you want to say?"

There was so much I might have persuaded myself to express at this last chance. That I was glad she was my mother. That I knew she loved me. That it was not her fault my father left us. That I had always loved and been thankful for her. That I wish I would have called her Mommy or Mom instead of only Mother.

You can do this, Nancy. Make it sound like truth.

Instead, "I want to say I'm sorry."

"And what are you sorry for?"

"I'm sorry you've lived your life in pain. That you've known so little happiness and joy. That I was not as devoted a daughter to you as you were to your mother." *Good start, Nancy. Stick with this tone.* "But there are also things I'm not sorry for." *Uh-oh.*

"And what would those be?" Still the bowed head, downcast eyes. *Could she not bear to look at me?*

"I'm not sorry I grew up. That I married John, whom you loved . . . perhaps more than you loved me . . . and we gave you two precious grandsons . . . the only enduring joy I knew you to have."

She does not refute my claim. *Perhaps this is going to go well.*

She says, "Did you ever realize how much I loved you?"

While a simple 'Yes' would have been the correct

176

answer, I proceed to say, "For many years, I thought I did. But then I recognized the difference between love and need. I believe what you thought was great love was actually great need — for things I was unable to give."

"You mean unwilling to give, don't you?"

At that, a warning bell in my brain. And yet I continue.

"Well, at some point, 'unable' did become 'unwilling.' It's hard for a teenager to raise a mother. I guess I finally stopped trying."

Is she wincing?

With clear cynicism, she asks, "And why was that?"

Don't go there! Perhaps you can still salvage this.

"Self-preservation, probably. John came along and he was stable and strong. I became determined — no matter what — to get married. To build a family."

You'd better stop now, Nancy. That's enough.

"But not like *my* family had been. This one had to be insular — secure and sane. I did what I believed I had to do to survive."

"In other words, you put yourself before me . . . knowing I still needed you so much."

You always needed me so much, Mother. When you woke me to say you had swallowed those pills after Kermit left us, you needed the ten-year-old me to waken the others to save you. You needed me to find my sustenance from school and friends, and in time I did. But then you wanted to live next door to your brutal boyfriend, Calvin, and you needed me to scrap my hard-won existence and move to a different school district — with you — beside him. You needed me to pick you up when he beat you down. You needed me to hate my father. And, at age fifteen, to accept a

177

stepfather and a new baby sister. And when I fell in love with both of them, and with our lives together, you needed me to start hating Fred like you did by then. You needed me to side with you in those dreadful midnight clashes you woke me up to referee.

I said none of those things. "I guess you could look at it that way, Mother."

"Well, I do. I sacrificed for you every day of my life, but you couldn't see your way to helping me."

Did she not remember the fourteen-year-old me beside her bed for days and nights while she sobbed that she was a failure of a mother — and how I argued and said it wasn't true — that she was a good mother and I loved her?

"Thank you for your sacrifices, Mother. For making Easter baskets for the neighborhood kids, and for teaching me to cook, and for polishing John's football shoes in high school and going to all his games when his own parents didn't, and for scraping together nineteen dollars for that had-to-have emerald green dress for football homecoming, and for never surrendering your steadfast goal for me . . . to have the money to go to college . . . and for finding Fred to be my stepfather, and for being the world's most devoted grandmother to the boys. I realize you sacrificed for me, and I am grateful."

I ask her a rhetorical question. "Did any of that make you happy?"

"You know it did."

"I guess I was never convinced. It wasn't enough. It didn't last. It didn't save you." My sincere reply.

Silence.

Then, a shaky deep breath. "Do you want to say

anything to me, Mother?"

Did she recall the times my grades and achievements made her proud . . . or only the ways I was an angry, sullen teenager? Would she admit that she never forgave me for not hating my father like she did and that she was devastated that I ended up not hating my stepfather, too? Would she tell me she remembered what I said at bedtime without fail after that fateful night at age ten: "Love you, see you in the morning?" That I would not go to bed until she answered yes? Or would she ask what had turned my heart to stone, and when?

She says only, "You were never there for me, Nancy."

I sigh. "I'm sorry that's what you think."

"It's what I know." She takes a pointed sip of her tea, cool now, like the air around us.

"We weren't the greatest match of mother and daughter, were we?" A novel idea—an unexplored volcano—bubbles to the surface of my mind.

"Maybe you and Kermit should never have married, Mother."

She glares at me with a face of granite, as if I had stumbled onto a certainty. It is a bolt of lightning to me, this notion that seems not new to her.

Twin sighs echo in unison. Then, "Enough."

Somehow, I refrain from reciting the lessons she had taught: trust no one, forgive even fewer. Or from "thanking" her for bequeathing to me the crushing weight of guilt.

But those legacies are not lost. I wrestle them even to this day.

In due time, and dramatically, my mother exits. With nary a goodbye.

Now, wouldn't a few simple "Thank you's . . . I love you's . . . Always have . . . always will . . ." have sufficed? After all, there was that golden, fragrant room . . . that chance for tenderness.

Alas, this one seems to be a drama that could not be scripted differently after all.

Sister to Sister

*O*t is December fourteenth. I sit alone beside a glittering pool awash in warm Florida sunshine. The water reflects the blue of the crystal sky above. Beyond the shimmering pool, gentle waves lap along a sandy shoreline. Typically a source of peace for me, today the waters do not soothe. This is my mother's birthday. Sighing as I dial, I call my sister . . . across the continent in Nebraska, her longtime home.

"Hi, Sissy," she says. "Is everything all right?"

We don't talk a lot. Neither of us likes the phone. Alison, fifteen years my junior, is an electronic communicator. Our usual contacts are by email or text or social media unless something is wrong. But we are always there for each other—any day, any time—at a moment's notice.

"It's Mother's birthday today," I say.

181

"Oh, right. Does that make you sad?"

"I always feel sad on her birthday. Do you?"

Alison hesitates. "To tell the truth, I don't really think about it."

"So different from me, especially now." Alison asks me to elaborate. She is a good listener.

"Well, she's on my mind more now, since I am writing this memoir—but always on her birthday, Christmas, Mother's Day. She and I never resolved things."

"I know, Sissy. Do you think that's your fault?"

"Well, I look at my friends who are close to their mothers, almost best friends, and I'm sorry it never happened for us. I can't really envision how we would have gotten there, but I always wonder what was wrong with me that I couldn't be friends with my own mother."

Always honest, Alison says, "I never really regretted that, or if I did, I got over it. And now I really don't think about her at all."

Alison and I have not talked in depth for some years, and now—through my writing—we have reconnected. She reads my stories, helps fill the blanks in my memory, gives me permission to write about her. For that, I am grateful. I want more. Like a journalist, I proceed.

"I picture the two of you like oil and water, always fighting, always in conflict. Will you tell me about your life with Mother after I moved away?"

"We were never close. I never relied on her for anything. I always wanted Dad."

"I guess that's why you have no feelings for Mother now."

"Right. In your critical years, you were surrounded by a whole world of dysfunction. You didn't have anybody stable to go to."

"I still feel guilty about our never achieving a caring relationship."

She sighs. "I hate that you feel so guilty all the time. You did everything you could for her, and more. We both had to cut ourselves off for our own survival."

She continues. "I don't think Mother was equipped to be a mother."

I catch my breath. Like a predatory shark, this irreverence has circled my head for years. I am awed that Alison feels it too. "What makes you say that?"

"We never bonded at all. If I needed something, I always went to Dad. I didn't feel a sense of safety or trust with Mom." Alison clears her throat. "I really don't think she ever loved me."

I stifle a gasp . . . the statement a near-sacrilege to my ears.

"Do you remember her being warm or caring with me when I was a baby?"

I frown. Moments go by as I rack my brain.

"Well, at fifteen, I probably wasn't paying that much attention. But I was thrilled to have a new baby sister. I showed you off to my friends and we were all in love with you. And so was Fred. I remember him holding you, cuddling, singing songs, telling silly stories. He couldn't wait to spend time with you, with his goofy grin and a twinkle in his eye."

I weigh my words, in the end, choosing honesty.

"But, to tell you the truth, I have no memory of Mother doing anything like that. I mean, I know she fed and bathed you and took good care of your needs. She dressed you up like a little doll. But I really can't picture much warmth or affection."

"That's what I thought," Alison says. "I think it was because she just wanted to be loved herself."

It dawned on me that my mother may have been jealous of her own daughter, for usurping attention she herself craved. Did this happen when I was born, too? Was Mother jealous of me for usurping Kermit's attention? The revelation is a jolt.

Alison switches gears. "Do you think, Sissy, because we were girls, we were competition for her?"

"What do you mean?"

"Well, I think she had a problem with women. Did you ever notice how she acted around men? How she always went after their attention?"

"You mean like the disastrous guys she hooked up with after she and Kermit divorced?" Alison had heard those stories.

"Not just them. She used to flirt with men all the time. Once, at a party, she really embarrassed me, flirting with the father of a friend of mine. Throwing herself at him, drunk, making a fool of herself. I really believe that at some point she was unfaithful to Dad."

I had never contemplated that, but the idea causes me to recall a conversation with my father. Over the years, I don't remember Kermit ever saying negative things about Mother. But in one particular discussion, his oblique comments suggested that she might have been unfaithful when he went away for the war, even before I was born. Though I did not question him, the idea burrowed into my mind. Alison's observation made me wish I had asked for details. I thought back, also, to how my mother mysteriously ended up in Fred's red convertible without anyone knowing how. Coincidence . . . or artful manipulation?

"Anyway," Alison says, "there always had to be drama. She lived for drama and conflict. And, of course, alcohol and drugs." Both Mother and Fred had abused alcohol and injectable pain killers for many years.

"I know Dad was no angel," Alison admits. "He drank, too, and supplied the drugs. And I think he thrived on their conflict as much as she did. But I could count on him to be there for me. Even when I was little, I went to him when I was hurt or needed anything. Mom always made me feel wrong and guilty. And she tried to empower herself by turning me against Dad."

I recall long nights of Mother trying to convince me how bad, mean, and wrong Fred was. Wanting me to take her side in the argument of the day. I can't remember what they fought about, but I can still feel the ferocity of the exchanges.

"Mother used to always say 'Why can't you be more like Nancy?' To hear her tell it, you were perfect."

The remark stuns me. "I'm amazed she said that. She was just guilting you. I disappointed her all the time. I could never do enough. If we visited, it was never long enough. If she came to see us in Pittsburgh, she would cry and get all depressed when it was time to leave; so then I would feel guilty. I didn't call her enough. She didn't say it until the end, but I knew I was never the daughter she needed me to be. That's where my remorse comes in." I shake my head. "If I gave an inch, it needed to be a mile — but even a mile wasn't enough. So I did the opposite — held her at arm's length. It makes me sad that I reacted that way."

Alison says, "I think Mother was a lot like her mother, Grandma Robb. Like an old-school wife and mother. Totally dependent upon a man for existence and self-worth. And Mother needed daughters who were like she was to Grandma. Always there, sacrificing her own life for Grandma's needs. She couldn't accept that we weren't like that. Our independence was a rejection of her. Because we were independent, we were disloyal."

I say, "Well, from my earliest memories, I knew Mother couldn't take living in another city, away from Grandma. She had to be in Kansas City, even if it meant giving up her marriage. Grandma always came first. You're right about that." Again, Alison had put into words things that had merely teased my mind. Another recollection surfaces.

"One time Mother and Fred and John and I were going to go to the lake for a weekend. We almost never went anywhere without some other family members. I was looking forward to being together, just the four of us. At the last minute, I found out that Grandma was going too. Mother had kept that detail from me."

"And you felt that Grandma was more important to her than you were," Alison says.

"Yes, and I protested. She called me selfish and

ungrateful . . . she couldn't see that I wanted to have some time to ourselves. And I was too proud and stubborn to tell her how I really felt. Mother called the trip off. I ended up begging and apologizing. We went and, of course, Grandma went along, like a martyr. I felt selfish and miserable the whole time."

"You weren't being the daughter she wanted you to be. You were looking forward to family time together, and she wanted her mother there. To you, that was rejection."

"Yeah. But I ended up feeling guilty, as always. Again, a selfish brat," I say. "Unlike you, I can't be objective. How did you turn your emotions off?"

"Well, I had Dad for support. And later, therapy," Alison continues. "When I finally cut myself off totally, I was in college, trying to afford tuition and living expenses. You and John had moved to Pittsburgh by then. Do you remember the piano that Grandpa Robb left to me?"

The piano had been in the living room after Grandpa's death. "I don't think I knew he left it to you."

"He did. And I needed it. Nobody but me played the piano, and I was going to sell it to help with my college expenses. Mother said no. She refused to let me have it. That was the final straw. I left home that day and never spoke to her again. Dad left her that night. That was the end for us."

We both know it was the beginning of the end for Mother, too.

"Mother wore her martyrdom like a cloak, every single moment of her life. It was her skin," Alison says. "Do you know why I didn't go away to college?" I didn't.

"She told me if I went away to school, she would kill

herself."

A wave of nausea overtakes me, stronger than the waves pulsing at the beach by my side. For an instant, I am a ten-year-old in a bottom bunk bed with a mother whispering good-bye in my ear. I want reach through the phone and take my sister in my arms, to shake a fist in fury at our mother, wherever she is. The revelation has sliced my psyche like a razor blade. I utter a strangled cry.

"One of my therapists told me something about guilt. She said guilt is displaced anger." Alison reminds me that neither guilt nor anger are healthy pursuits.

We fall silent. Our sighs are heavy. As though in need of oxygen, we move to gentler reflections.

Alison asks, "Do you remember any times when she was happy?"

"Only when she had a job. I remember her at her best when she worked at Ken-A-Vision and you were little. Or when her grandsons were born."

"You're right. And she was a different person when she worked at the medical center after you moved away. Happy, funny, self-confident. Dad and I begged her not to quit that job."

"Why did she quit?"

"Because they wouldn't give her time off to visit you guys in Pittsburgh."

"Oh, wow. She was always better when she was working. In one of the last conversations I ever had with her, I urged her to get a job, even part time. But she refused. Said she was too weak and sick."

We agree that our mother was as smart and capable

as she was manipulative. Successful at every job she held, yet unable to conquer her own insecurities — finally falling victim to depression, anger, drugs, alcohol. And we lament how the treatments of the day failed her.

"If therapies and drugs had been different 'back in the day,' we might have had a totally different mother to remember."

With that, our conversation stalls. I am exhausted. Weak.

"Love you, Sissy," Alison says, calling me by the name she always does. A name I love. "I'm so glad you are writing your book. We can talk any time, and you can write anything you want about me."

"Love you too, Al."

We end our call. I fall deep in thought, comforted by things Alison confirmed, shaken by others she revealed. What a regrettable cycle for three generations of women — grandmother, mother, two daughters. Not close, never happy, left with wounds and scars. Was this the reason I once prayed for only sons? Was I not sure I could trust myself to raise a daughter? Yet now, I treasure my two lovely daughters-in-law — who are my friends — and a precious granddaughter who fills my heart with joy. And my sister with her own beautiful, loving daughter . . . a dear niece.

On this December fourteenth, Mother's birthday, I choose beauty. The sun warms my heart and dries my tears. I recognize that a sorry cycle has run its course. I say amen.

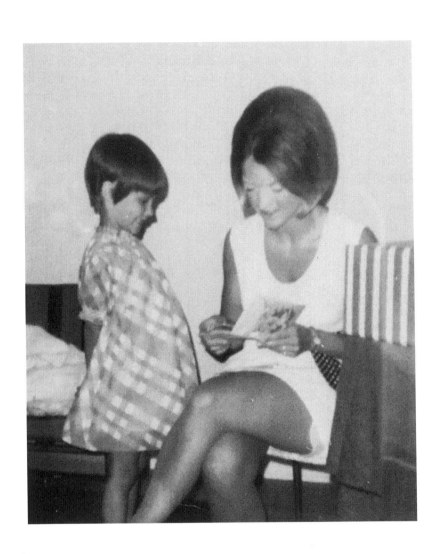

Windows

It is said that the eyes are windows to the soul. The girl, now a woman, thinks about eyes. She recalls the eyes of her parents.

The craggy brown eyes of her father — once crinkling with laughter and love — indecipherable upon his departure to another home, another family. And the eyes of her mother. Deep brown and brimming. Dimmed by divorce. Deadened from shock treatments. Purple and blackened by the fists of a poorly chosen suitor. Brightened upon a second marriage and the birth of a new baby daughter. Turned red, hostile, as that marriage crumbles. Aglow for a time with love and pride for two cherished baby grandsons. But defeated and darkened once and for all — drowned in waves of misery — upon the final failure of love and marriage.

In a twist of irony, the brown-eyed parents each passed a recessive gene to their daughter . . . the daughter they called "Nancy with the Laughing Face." Green eyes that, to the world, sparkle and glimmer. Eyes that, at the same time, conceal something sinister under their layer of laughter.

The daughter's improbable green eyes suppress a secret . . . a demon known as envy. Envy for those whose fathers are present and mothers are whole. For those who wake feeling confident, secure, hopeful. For those whose eyes do not spout unbidden tears at ill-timed moments. For those who are free to be less than perfect—who do not quake at the possibility of failure. Envy for those who trust well and love without fear of loss. And envy for those who need not bury jaded jealousies behind the veiled windows to their souls.

Sounds of Silence

*T*wo words. Two sisters. Two years. Two families, torn in two.

"Ungrateful brat!"

Like buckshot, Aunt Julie's words burst at me as I entered the living room through the patio door. I glimpsed my mother, cowering behind her, shoulders raised at ear level as though to muffle the sounds of the assault. Mother stared, not at me, but toward the floor.

Aunt Julie had been in the house with my mother while I practiced cheers outside. At the ambush, my head jerked back. I was a junior in high school, circling within the happy orbit of an intact family, back at my beloved Raytown High School. Living, for once, what felt like a normal existence.

My aunt stepped closer. "Just who do you think you are?"

With widening eyes and gaping mouth, I stumbled backward. I had been witness to my aunt's hair-trigger temper before and knew to stay out of the line of fire.

The harangue halted mid-sentence when my stepfather came in from work and placed himself between me and my red-faced aunt.

"What the hell is going on?" Fred's voice sounded like thunder. He, too, had been a victim of Julie's random assaults, more than once . . . usually accompanied by liberal doses of alcohol, as may have been the case that day.

Aunt Julie's heated reply, her litany of grievances, bounced like a ping pong ball from Fred's chest. I had gone deaf, oblivious to the details, but I heard his measured response.

"This conversation is over, Julie. You can leave." Once again, Fred had rescued me. My fleeting thought was that this would not make Mother happy.

"If I do, it's going to be the last you see of me. And, mark my words, you'll rue the day you ignored me about this one here." She shook a finger at my face. I flinched.

My aunt turned to my mother. "Do you hear me, Vi? I mean this."

Mother swallowed deeply. "You'd better go now, Julie."

Julie huffed out, leaving us in silence. I still recall my shock at Mother's "Sophie's Choice." Had she really sided with me, and Fred, against her sister?

Though in the past it was not unusual for Aunt Julie's verbal assaults to require little or no provocation, Fred looked at Mother and asked, "What brought that on?"

But I piped right up. "I just walked in the door and she let me have it. I have no idea what I did." Turning to my mother with a shrug, I wondered why she remained mute, staring again at the floor. Was she, too, in shock at her choice? Or did her silence signal something more? Guilt? Complicity? Without a word, she left for the kitchen. An aroma of meatloaf soon reached us in the living room.

I was not party to any follow-up discussion of the incident. We ate dinner in silence . . . a silence like the one that began that day and lasted for the next two years. Aunt Julie stayed true to her word. The sisters ceased to communicate.

My teenage ego bristled. I wasn't the perfect daughter, but I didn't get into trouble, had nice friends, and made good grades. The same could not be said of Gretchen, Aunt Julie's own daughter, who was flaming her way through her teens in ways I could barely fathom. At our school, I cringed at oft-repeated tales of my cousin's outrageous escapades. It was not unusual to hear, "And you're Gretchen Green's cousin? Wow. You two are nothing alike."

Yet my aunt had lashed out at me? Crazy. I could tell her a thing or two about troublesome teens.

The divided family festered . . . Mother bereft, Fred resolute, me stunned. The years took a toll on my mother — she who valued her family of origin above all else in the world — who had been used to speaking with her sister at least once a day. She wilted like a flower untended. And the gray circles which grew ever deeper below her eyes mirrored a dark well of guilt now invading my head and

195

heart.

It took a family tragedy, the illness and death of their mother, Grandma Robb, to reverse the effects of those unthinkable years. In a wake of grief, the sisters bonded again, and their shroud of silence lifted forever. The effects, however, were not expunged.

Echoes of two years of family suppression, with me at the core, rang on in my head. Grandma's death did not mute them. And nothing ever silenced a nagging question in my mind. Was my volatile aunt merely the messenger that day . . . delivering my own mother's wrath toward me?

Sophie's Choice, indeed.

Patches

*A*nd now I am a memoirist, composing a quilt of words for my mother. Rummaging through a treasure trove of memories—calling them forth to be bound with fragile filament and handled with care. Like the heart of a loved one.

Picture a square with a white background, upon which is embossed a red lobster . . . her favorite restaurant. The last meal we ate out together was at the Red Lobster. She ordered stuffed shrimp, her favorite. She smiled.

A red and green patch is bigger and brighter than the others. Christmas was her favorite holiday. This fleecy shape is warm and comforting.

Santa's whiskers prickle from a dazzling white square—like the whiskery traces she drew on an empty glass, so I would think Santa had drunk the milk we left on the hearth. The cookies were gone too, except for the last one, with a big bite out of it.

A pink, yellow and green square mimics woven strips of construction paper for homemade Easter baskets. Baskets filled with shiny Easter grass, candy eggs, jellybeans. Distributed by us to friends in our Rochester neighborhood on frosty Easter eves. This square smells of sweetness, generosity.

The mud-hued brown square calls to mind the footprints of the Easter bunny, lovingly stamped in the stealth of Easter eve across our entry hall floor and living room carpet. Footprints leading to a huge overflowing Easter basket . . . filled with love for a wide-eyed daughter.

One golden square resembles a grained piece of wood, like the oaken timeout stool upon which I sat in our Rochester kitchen, with the oven timer ticking off a penance imposed by my father. When Mother crept in, the ticks of the timer would whir in triple speed for an instant. As she sneaked out, the bell would ding, ending my foreshortened punishment and cementing our little secret.

A royal blue square sports a crisp white trim, the colors of the Raytown High School Bluejay. Embroidered upon this square is a pair of shiny black football shoes — those shoes she polished after every game — the brightest cleats in the locker room, and the only ones with little good-luck notes inside. She was in the stands for all his games and once, when John scored an exciting touchdown, she wet her pants.

The fleecy white square represents lamb's wool. "A lamb is small, a sheep is big," she explained to me, at age seventeen, on a ride in the country in a red convertible. We laughed with, not at, her. This square is oft repeated across the quilt, just as the incongruous quote was in our family.

An emerald green swatch comes from an unaffordable nineteen-dollar homecoming dress. Somehow, she found a way. I wore it to the homecoming dance with the football captain, my future husband.

A pale avocado square represents wedding memories. Silky, like her mother-of-the-bride ensemble — reflecting a pained smile. On it, tears shimmer, some for joy, more for loss. And a frilly avocado frock, worn by the younger daughter, that impish five-year-old flower girl, grinning gaily as she gains a beloved brother, husband to her precious "Sissy."

One square is crafted of yellow and white gingham plaid, like the gift boxes from Raytown's boutique children's shop. Boxes bulging with extravagant purchases for her grandsons. Adorable outfits, precious shoes. Purchases she could not afford, yet nothing was too dear for her darlings. From each item hung a visible price tag that I removed — feeling guilty for her excess.

A solid yellow square is adorned with two cigarettes, reminiscent of a day when she was babysitting. Her two young charges had found a gallon of house paint and smeared a large canary-colored swath across our field-stone house. I returned home to see her scrubbing paint, brandishing a garden hose and smoking two cigarettes at once. Most of the paint came off; the gilded memory remains forever.

A purple patch is for juice, from early morning to late at night. Grape juice liberally laced with an invisible, odorless destroyer . . . the vicious vodka whose power corrupted what should have been her golden years.

A mossy green square recalls a lonely lake on a frigid October afternoon. A lake which conceals tragedy beneath its murky surface.

On each corner of the quilt sits a deep gray patch—the haunting color of unmade memories and precious breaths never to be drawn.

Every square of the perimeter is white. Small and white, embroidered in red. An endless border of tiny broken hearts.

In the center of the quilt there sits a large, streaked patch—a rosy square like the sky following a vibrant sunset. And an inscription, authored by Teresa Shanti, which reads ". . . I'm sorry for the unhealed parts of me that in turn hurt you. It was never a lack of love for you. Only a lack of love for myself."

The sun does not set on the center square. Rather, a full moon rises and glints across a dusky ocean, transmitting unforgettable beams into the infinite scarlet sky.

Another Mother

$\mathcal{T}$he pediatrician looked at the baby with a gentle smile. "What's going on with this little guy?"

Well prepared, I handed him a thick sheaf of notes. He fanned through the pages.

"What is all of this?" His tone sounded inappropriate toward a dutiful mom such as myself.

"My mother says it's important to make a note of everything so that you'll know what the baby has been doing."

I nodded at the pages where I had charted every single detail of my child's existence, on sheet after sheet of darling yellow-and-white polka-dot note paper which matched his crib bumper-pads. Weeks of day-by-day, minute-to-minute notations: eating (when, what, how much, duration), sleeping (when, where, how long), peeing (when, color, odor), pooping (when, how much, color, odor, consistency), crying (duration, intensity . . . of the baby's crying jags — not mine).

I detected a strangled look on the doctor's face. He must have been thinking it was no wonder the baby was there for excessive crying and colic.

"I don't want you to write one more thing about this child — unless he is running a fever, gasping for breath, or covered in a rash. NO MORE LOGS!"

He thrust the pages at me. I'm pretty sure he would rather have ripped them in half. I remained silent, red as a beet, as he examined my son.

We left the office with some kind of tonic for the baby. I think if he could have done so, that doctor would have given me an enormous bottle of Valium . . . or the name of a foster parent for my child.

It was 1974. Earlier that year, another birth had occurred. The birth of a 'Mamau.'

Mamau arrived the day John and I announced our pregnancy with our first child. Mother chose the moniker for herself, from the French (a heritage of which we had not a drop). This ecstatic grandmother-to-be shifted into a higher gear than did my own hormones. She launched into spending sprees — baby furniture, bibs, blankets, bottles, bumper pads. And books by "experts." But I soon reckoned the actual expert was Mother herself, a self-anointed guru of baby care.

Her advice flowed freely and often. I was told in no uncertain terms that the NUMBER ONE most important thing with a newborn was to keep him on a schedule. Never feed him more than every two hours; stretch that to four hours as soon as possible. Wake him up in the daytime if he's sleeping when he's supposed to be eating. Don't pick him up when he cries . . . you'll spoil him. No matter what, don't let him get his days and nights mixed up. And NUMBER TWO—document every moment of his life. This mother of mine, who herself had frozen in fear—needing rescue—at my birth, was an overnight authority on how to take care of a baby.

Sufficiently obsessive in my own right, and with that set-up, I was somewhat daunted at our son's birth. Because he has declined to make anything more than a cameo appearance in this narrative, suffice it to say that the poor child's nerve-wracked mother (me) did him no favors. My mother's admonitions rang in my ears, drowning my own maternal instincts. I behaved like a camp counselor minus the whistle, shifting from activity to activity whether the baby was on board or not. Chaos ensued. And yet, Mother always reported that he was an angel when in her care. Never a problem of any kind. And though my sister, Alison, a teenage witness at the time, has since refuted these reports, their impact left me faltering. I questioned my every move. Somehow, I was failing 'Routines and Schedules,' 'Consistency and Care.' The one thing I felt I could do to satisfaction was document, document. Had I been set up for failure? To do more poorly than my mother had done?

Some would call it sabotage.

Those yellow-and-white polka-dot pages still exist, secreted away in our son's baby book (itself another marvel of detail). When his brother came along three years later, he somehow survived infancy without a daily log. Almost without a baby book. Mamau's gig was up. I tried to convince myself she had only meant well.

By then, Mother and I had shared the best of times and the worst of them . . . our own "springs of hope, winters of despair." There were the early years I think of as the Mom Years, though I don't remember ever calling her that. The Cinderella-sequin times—with Smokey and Inky and Easter baskets and pogo sticks—years that leave a glow in the mind. Then came the Mother Years—those troublesome days of darkness and dawn and darkness again. But also, with their positives and negatives, there were the Mamau Years.

However unnerving my mother was to me, she became a world-class grandmother to our sons. Everything a grandmother is supposed to be: doting, caring, loving, you name it. Fun, funny, playful—selfless at long last. Over-indulgent, for sure, absent discipline, of course . . . as is so often the way with grandparents, to the universal bane of the poor parents. And though much too dramatic then, I now understand—as a grandmother myself—the sobbing goodbyes, the much-maligned absences.

Notwithstanding the downsides, I give thanks that our sons knew the Mamau they did. The highest achievement of motherhood, it seems to me, is a legacy of love and care. My mother left that, and more, for her cherished grandsons. I can only hope that, as a grandmother myself, I will do as well.

An Ode to Water

*W*hat is more sensual than water? To the eyes, it glistens, sparkles, ripples, and shines. The sight of water mesmerizes . . . fostering images of the teeming world of life below. And the sound of water! It can roar or whisper, boom or lap, crash . . . or glitter in profound silence. Again, mesmerizing. Then there is the smell of water. Whether you find it salty or seaweedy, fresh or fishy, clean or dank, water emits a primordial smell . . . eerily embryonic. Leaving you to crave the feel of it. To be enveloped within a silky, foamy, tender caress or a powerful embrace. Water invites you to splash in it, to ride its rising and falling waves, to wash in its bubbly foam. To be buoyed by its majesty.

Water is a principal character in my life story.

Troubled Waters

One summer, my parents rented a vacation cabin beside nearby Lake Canandaigua. I took my pet—a tiny painted turtle. We placed his glass globe on the windowsill in my bedroom, a spot with a view. And the little guy, whiffing freedom nearby, crawled right out the window without so much as a backward glance. This turtle memory still summons a wistful smile, but another Canandaigua recollection does not. Unbeknownst to me, on this trip, my father had resolved that I would learn to swim.

He approached my training with a jaunty grin, most likely believing that swimming would be a cinch for the daughter of two accomplished swimmers. From our lakeside cabin, he led me—a stumbling eight-year-old—down a pebbled path and into what proved to be icy water. Sharp, slippery rocks comprised the shoreline. As I waded in, my feet wobbled and slid. The water seized me with fingers of ice. Waves from passing boats batted us back and forth. My father barked directions for moves and maneuvers. He demonstrated the actions I was to perform, undeterred by my plaintive protests. Steadfastly immobile — unable to comply — I fought to remain upright. After a time, my frowning father turned his muscled back and stalked up the pathway. I negotiated my solitary way out of the water and across the rocky shore. With hanging head and chattering teeth, I returned to the cottage amid a loud lament.

"I give up. She's all yours now." My father did not suffer defeat gladly. Mother shook her head, lips pursed.

Kermit Hill was an athlete. He played tennis and basketball in high school. He was a golfer. I had witnessed his impressive ability to beat a clock by transferring balloons over a net with razor blades. Foremost, however, my father was a swimmer. To be precise, a former World War II Navy frogman. In his autobiography, he chronicled grueling training in Fort Pierce, Florida, and Maui, Hawaii. His tour of duty took him to the Pacific Theater, where he was a member of Underwater Demolition Team #18. Those brave men carried out their final hazardous duty missions below the churning waters of Tokyo Bay, in murky depths, perhaps nose-to-nose with sharks and sea creatures, warships hulking above. The frogmen flippered down through treacherous waters in search of the live enemy mines which lurked in shadowy seascapes. Their job — to defuse the deadly mines, preparing for the arrival of the USS Missouri, the vessel upon which the WWII peace treaty would be signed. I have envisioned my father completing his work—then kicking up and up, breaking the shimmering surface of the water—into blue skies and sunshine. Into a deep breath of fresh air. Into peace.

I have viewed my father's pictures and plaques in the Navy Seal Museum in Fort Pierce, a scant ten miles north of my current winter home. In the museum are dioramas of those early Seals—the WWII frogmen—wiry men in skimpy briefs with archaic air tanks on their bare backs, flippers on their feet, and belts with knives around their waists.

Yes, my father, Kermit Hill, was a swimmer, but at age eight, I knew almost nothing of this. I knew only that he was determined that his daughter would learn to swim.

Mother was a swimmer as well. A sputtering scene from a spotty sepia home movie plays across my mind—a scene in which my mother, young and lithe, chases me, her golden-haired toddler, along a sandy beach into frothy surf. I wore a pink swim outfit with puffy pants and a heart-shaped top lined with ruffles, thighs chubby even then. Mother later told me she almost drowned at Rehoboth Beach that year, in what would now be called a rip current, but that her strong swimming skills saved her. In later years, I watched Mother swim in pools and lakes, slicing through water like a sleek, shining otter in a signature sidestroke. Always graceful. Tan and glistening. A beautiful swimmer. But again, at age eight, I knew only that my parents both could swim.

The failed 'teach-Nancy-to-swim' vacation ended. Back home in Rochester, Mother took me to the YMCA for a series of lessons. There, I slithered into an immense pool in a steamy room with other young recruits. I did not make rapid progress. I remember bedtime lectures about swimming—gruff admonitions by my father about the need for swimming skills. A bit about his frogman days. His list of all the reasons I was wrong to be afraid. Gentle expressions of support and encouragement from my mother.

With each lesson, I performed single components of the swimming stroke, but when asked to put them all together, I clung like a barnacle to the side of the pool. But one night, a swimming dream came into my head. In it, I swam like my graceful mother, my frogman father—conquering that steamy YMCA pool, free of fear, amazing my instructors. I awoke in eager anticipation of my swim lesson that afternoon.

At this point in the series of lessons, our task was to jump off a low diving board, touch the bottom of the pool, kick up and rise, then paddle to the side without help. To date, I had not accomplished this feat. But on the day after my dream, I climbed to the board and jumped right in. I felt myself sinking to the bottom where my toes met tile. With my heart pounding, I ran out of breath. But then came a sense of air—not water—filling my lungs. After the lesson, I told my parents that, at six feet deep, I gulped a breath of air beneath the surface.

"It really happened. It really did," I said. Fearful no longer, I finished the course and graduated a swimmer. With rolling eyes, my parents sighed.

Even after acquiring the fundamentals of swimming, I do not recall a fondness for water in those early years. My family lived only a mile from Lake Ontario, where frigid winds and glaring rays of the seaside sun seared my eyes and chilled my bones. In those years, our visits to the beach were far less gratifying than my enjoyment of water in its solid form . . . upon which I could ice-skate.

There were no more family lake vacations on which to practice and apply my new abilities. Instead, there was the divorce. My swimming skills, such as they were, went with me to Kansas City, where Mother and I moved. My father remained in Rochester, building a new family and house with a terraced yard and sparkling pool. His stepchildren became expert swimmers.

In Kansas City I swam when necessary, well enough to get me through my teenage summers without drowning in front of friends at the community pool. As the years unfolded, though I remained only a passable swimmer, I found I craved being in or on the water. Sun-drenched hours in pools and lakes highlighted the summer months. Slathered with baby oil and iodine, I accrued impressive sunbathing credentials, a golden tan and a lifetime supply of freckles. Though I loved bow-riding best, somewhere along the line I learned to water ski. Boating and water sports became my favorite activities. I was drawn to the water, perhaps as a part of my genetic code.

It became a virtual love affair . . . my devotion to water. I found that water aroused every fiber of me. Yet, given my aquatic history over the years, this passion seemed somewhat curious.

Eventually I reached sixty, the age at which Mother died. For many people, outliving one's same-sex parent is a milestone ... an accomplishment which evokes potent emotions, inspires new goals. For me, this was the start of the "golden years."

I embarked upon a search for a grown-up sport to lubricate my aching bones and joints. While wintering in Florida, I tried swimming. A neighbor taught me how to do laps without sputtering and choking. Swimming became my compulsion. Now, some years later, if a week goes by without a few sessions of lap swimming, I feel depressed and deprived. I organize and lead aerobic water workouts in my neighborhood. I am in water more days than not. Even from afar, water soothes my every sense. Whether sitting beside a crashing surf, observing the gleaming shaft of a full moon rising over the ocean, or gazing from on high at a majestic water view, I am fulfilled. Yet there is a darker dimension to my kinship with water.

It was 1985. I was an adult—married, with children of my own, living in Pennsylvania. That year, in the water, my mother completed her lifelong quest ... that which she had first attempted when I was ten. A task at which she had failed, several times and in various ways, over the decades.

Now divorced for the second time and without a home of her own, Mother lived with my aunt and uncle beside a little Raytown neighborhood lake. On a gray October afternoon, she took a cab to the deserted end of that lake, telling the driver she was headed to meet a man. With clues from cab company records, the family learned of her deed and retraced her steps on that fateful day.

My mother had not gone to meet a man, at least not one of this Earth. Instead, in the chill air of fall, she filled her coat pockets with rocks and walked into the watery depths, never to emerge. It was her final shocking act on this Earth, and she left goodbyes for no one.

Then, and for a long time thereafter, my feelings submerged as if in a submarine. I didn't reveal Mother's manner of death, concocting some story about succumbing to various conditions. "Suicide by drowning" was a phrase I could neither contemplate nor utter. People stopped asking.

Yet my love affair with water lives on. At times, it engulfs my mind. Sometimes, when swimming laps, I think of my parents. The one who swam and the one who drowned. But when I glide beneath the water's surface, as it surrounds and embraces me, I think not of how my father, the frogman, paddled out of my life early on, leaving me high and dry. Nor do I recall my mother's dark and watery demise.

I think of bravery . . . and of my father — with nothing more than swim fins, bulky air tanks, and a belt of tools and sheathed knives — plunging into the churning depths of an ocean bristling with live enemy mines. I contrast my mother's uncertain courage in the water. From what resources could a person — a mother and grandmother — summon the resolve to walk into a lake with pockets of rocks — to take a last breath, not of air, but of water? Did she fear that, as happened at Rehoboth Beach, her strong swimming skills would once again extricate her from depths she now desired to inhabit forever? Was hers a peaceful end, a release of pain, or did she panic at the end and try to change the course of her decision? After numerous thwarted attempts to go by way of pills, how did she come upon the idea of drowning herself? Of what, or whom, were her last thoughts? Did she see in her last act, as did I, an ironic parallel to my father and his bravado in the water?

I recently shared some of these musings with my cousin Gary. Though he had no answers to the many unknowns, he told me of a strange photo he had found among his mother's posthumous possessions . . . an old picture. A yellowing photo of two young women in their teens. The two sisters—his mother and mine—are standing on a cliff overlooking the sea. Handwritten on the back, in spidery script, is an unsigned note which says, "A good place to commit suicide." Could these have been my mother's words, her thoughts . . . even as a teenager?

So many mysteries. Yet still I swim. And on sunny days, when I descend into the glistening blue water of a sparkling pool, there shimmers a grid—a checkerboard of gold. It enmeshes me in a netted cloak of well-being. And my questions, without answers, dissolve.

GLIMMERS OF GOLD

"The two most important days in your life are the day you are born and the day you find out why."

Mark Twain

Many Moons

$\mathcal{I}$t was twenty-four years after that full moon above a frosty front lawn in Missouri — where Mother was saved — when she waded into the deserted end of the little Raytown lake, never to return. Concluding not just her life, but a tortured chapter of mine, as well. I do not know if there was a full moon — or any moon at all — on that decisive night.

And now, a girl no longer, I am curiously and compulsively drawn, not only to water, but to the full moon. Every full moon. Marking the dates on my calendar, I alert my friends. With loved ones and libations each month, I watch the golden orb rise over a beach or a firepit or the mountains or my back patio, wherever I might be. With a quickening pulse, I witness the awe-inspiring event, rarely missing a month. When at the beach, a regular entourage of moon-watchers, summoned by me, greets the fiery orange ball on the horizon as it ascends over the water. Breaking waves twinkle as if crowned with tiny dancing flames. The rising moon sends its searing shaft of light across the foamy surf into the depths of my heart and takes my breath away. But no longer does my blood run cold.

I do not fault the moon for my lost childhood. Quite the opposite, I wonder if the fullness of the moon somehow nourishes the sturdy peace of mind which fortifies me as an adult . . . a peace which releases me to acknowledge and write, after over sixty years, the tale of my tattered childhood.

Epiphany

$\mathcal{T}$hey say the things you don't know can't hurt you. Until you know them. This I have learned.

Perhaps it was fate, serendipity, divine providence — maybe even the brilliant, almost-full moon the previous night — that led my curiosity to *kchistory.org*, a website on which I unveiled the Paseo High School yearbook of 1941. Having reached me so late along the path to completion of my memoir, I feared this discovery might change everything.

With quaking fingers, I scanned through grainy pages, beginning with the image of a stately limestone-clad edifice towering atop a tall hill at 47th Street and The Paseo in Kansas City, Missouri. Sure enough, this was their school. I had stumbled into a digital facsimile of Paseo's fifteenth yearbook issue, the one that chronicles the senior year of Violet Robb and Kermit Hill. During an hour's fearsome foray into these pages—at age seventy-two—I met my parents for what seemed like the very first time. As if they were reaching out to me from years gone by. I trembled in anticipation of what I would learn.

Searching alphabetically among the senior class pictures, I found Kermit Hill. Crisp-collared and impeccably groomed, he raised his chiseled chin and presented a confident half-grin to the camera. Neatly shorn hair and full dark eyebrows framed brown eyes that gazed afar, as if toward a preferred future. The editor's description read:

HILL, KERMIT E. — *Kermit says he will go anywhere but Junior College next year. He was not so set against Paseo, though, as he was President of El Ateneo and Los Parlantes and was a member of Keats and the Quill and Scroll.*

Further wanderings through the file took me to a picture in which my father looks at the camera—at me—with a somber expression from the top row of the National Honor Society. I came to a likeness of him as a featured Editor of the Paseo Press, and to an image that gave me chills—that of Kermit standing shoulder to shoulder with my mother on the Debate Team, their four eyes looking out as if directly into my two. Below that arresting shot, I read that "the student body of Paseo had an opportunity to become familiar with the oratorical powers of six of the debaters in an assembly. The question for the debate was 'Resolved: That the powers of the Federal Government should be increased.'" I read that one of the three debaters on the affirmative side was Kermit Hill. With an ironic grin, I thought of a long-standing absolute . . . my father's lifelong dedication to the principles of conservatism and the

Republican Party ... and how that staunch blood had flowed directly to him from the veins of his own father. I have to believe that Clarence Hill did not attend, or perhaps even know of, his son's argument in this schoolhouse debate.

Further along in the annual, when I saw Kermit standing with the Keats Literary Society as its treasurer, a sorry recollection surfaced. Despite his stated intentions to the contrary, he did, indeed, end up going to Junior College the following year. In his autobiography, I had read that his family's tight finances allowed only for his older brother, not Kermit, to go away to school.

Like a hungry bear after a long winter nap, I devoured more of this priceless relic. I approached the primary intention of my quest—the class picture of my mother—Violet Robb. With a sharp intake of breath, I viewed a timid smile and deep brown eyes laced with just a hint of mischief. Lustrous dark curls framed her face, twining into a topknot crowned with a whimsical ribbon. About her, the editor had written:

ROBB, VIOLET MARY— *Vi's tender heart is evidenced by the fact that she wants to be a nurse. Our peppy cheerleader will have to calm down a bit, however, in order to take up hospital training. She kept the minutes for the Zetas, was song leader for El Ateneo, and has been a student council representative.*

The narrative staggered me. I blotted tears from my eyes at the thought that Mother was so "tender," even in high school, that the quality was immortalized in her yearbook. I, too, had known my mother to be tender—yet reading such words penned over seventy years ago took my

221

breath away. And learning for the first time that she was peppy . . . a leader . . . that she wanted to be a nurse? These revelations, unknown to me, unleashed a fresh batch of tears. I wished the world to stop spinning — to take me back in time — so I could reach out to that captivating girl looking toward me from the pictures of the Zetas, Spanish Club, Debate Team, Student Council, and Mr. Richardson's homeroom in her cheerleader uniform . . . this person I never knew. I envisioned taking her by the shoulders and whispering the Paseo High School motto into her ear: "Remember who you are." I wanted to mother *her*.

And thus, on a rainy afternoon in front of a flickering screen, I met my parents — Kermit and Violet, high-school sweethearts — two talented young people going about their lives with happy naivete, just as the larger world, in 1941, was about to come unglued. Two carefree youths facing an uncertain future — bound to one another — intent on making positive contributions to their domain, Paseo High School.

It humbled me to ponder that, in just six short years, these youngsters would marry — part company as one went off to fight a war and the other went back home to her parents — then rejoin, settle in a strange new city, bear a child of their own. All by age twenty-three. Were these the pressures that first splintered their connection to each other . . . that dimmed my mother's twinkling eyes . . . that fissured their bond until, ten years later, it snapped forever — as did my mother herself? For her, the world came unglued not in 1942, but in 1957. Her sweetheart gone, her life dream over, her daughter a sudden solitary obligation.

I sit amid this treasure trove of fractured family lore,

feeling more like a protective parent than a deserted daughter. Had I stumbled upon these artifacts long ago, how different might my perspective have been? Likely, I would not have been considerably swayed by the profile of my father. I've always known that he went on to achieve his potential and live out his dream after leaving us in his wake. No, his high-school persona is not surprising. But to have discovered my mother as a peppy, confident leader in a milieu of over 2,600 classmates? I want to know so much more. If I were to write another letter to her, it would be filled with questions: *You were so capable, talented, caring . . . why did you not pursue nurses' training? Who and what deflated your reserves of confidence and cheer? When did that mischievous twinkle depart your deep brown eyes?* Finally, and most unsettling to me, *What prevented you from allowing me, your child, to learn who you once were behind the ragged cloak you wore in your role as wife and mother?*

At age seventy-two, the circumstance of being newly introduced to my parents has been uncanny. And the notion that Kermit and Violet somehow reached out to find me—and not the other way around—is positively eerie; I cannot shake the irony. Nor can I squelch a surreal notion in my mind—this wish to dial back time and say to these handsome teenagers, "Choose a different adventure! Choose happiness." But then, of course, where would that leave me?

With a sigh, I close my eyes and ponder my discoveries. I allow them to wash over me like a gentle, cleansing wave. Atop the wave rides an enhanced version of the two souls who brought me into this world . . . not changing everything, but altering some of my reality. I tell myself to refocus from sadness and regret to new dimensions—pride, pleasure, gratitude. Pride in who Kermit and Violet once were. Pleasure in knowing that Mother did, in fact, experience sustained joy in her life, as brief as it may have been. Gratitude that I may now summon another dimension of Mother's past . . . one which lightens the darkness that shadows so many of her later years. And further gratitude that it wasn't too late to have met a mother who was once a peppy, confident leader—with a whimsical bow atop her bouncy brown curls.

And so, I move on . . . unsettled, yet comforted, by the yearbook from Paseo High School, 1941. Still, I feel an ache, a caution. I tell myself, as the adage says, "Don't trip over something that's behind you."

I will watch my step.

EPILOGUE

For just over twenty years, my last name was Hill. Though I was born into the Hill family, my physical years within that family numbered less than ten. Our family's navigations among the peaks and valleys of life were brief. Our paths diverged.

Today, with my precious brown-eyed pup, Bentley, I walk the gentle hills of a rolling meadow trail in western Pennsylvania. This time I contemplate neither the other brown eyes I have known, nor my family of origin—the Hills. I am savoring different hills this afternoon.

On our climb, we are bordered by wispy wildflowers which bob their heads along our path, tickling Bentley's nose. A shimmering blue sky blankets us from on high. Feathery clouds dust our vistas. Bentley is a gentle walker; he stops and sniffs, sniffs and stops, marking the path lest

227

we lose our way as we return. I delight in the summer breeze which cools my dewy brow as we ascend to the crest of a rise. Our path then descends into a verdant valley.

It occurs to me that today's walk is a metaphor for life itself: a series of hills. Some, like those in this meadow, present gentle ascents and declines which may be traversed with ease. Yet I know that life's steeper inclines can reward with breathtaking vistas on top. And extreme declines might cause you to stumble, but then come flat plains upon which you will regain your footing.

The hills of this life are pierced with tunnels—short tunnels speckled with visible light, longer tunnels which wind and snake, dark and foreboding. But at the end of every tunnel, no matter how long or short, a light shines forth—pointing to the way out.

I think how I have faltered at the foot of certain hills in my life, convinced that I could not reach the top. Afraid to try. I remember others on which I lost my way, going up or coming down. I recall, in my younger years, schussing across craggy slopes with wind in my hair and waxed skis as my feet. Now I climb grassy inclines aided by spikes on my shoes and a putter in my hand. The day may come when I need a ride up or a supporting arm on the way down. But there will always be another incline. The paths of one's life are never flat. I do not wish that they were.

Losing my place in the Hill family was the steepest ascent I ever faced. Others have been easier. I recall the hills and valleys of a cherished career among children and those who care for them—peaking as I took my seat on a bench on a school playground before departing for retirement. A bench that displays a plaque bearing my name, inscribed with the words: "Principal, Teacher, Friend."

The tunnels of my life have glimmered with guiding lights—a good husband, two matchless sons, precious grandbabies, loyal dogs, beautiful friends, replacement body parts for those that wore out. In luck and love, I reached a lofty vista, a grand peak upon which dawned a fiftieth wedding anniversary celebration ... peopled with those I hold most dear ... my lifelong husband, sons, daughters-in-law, grandchildren, relatives, special friends. I am ever grateful for the hills and tunnels of this life.

In eternity, I wish for a bench upon a stately summit where I can savor a view of the hills and valleys of this stunning Earth. Of course, I also hope to survey an expanse of water—a dappled lake or an ocean's crashing surf, lighted by the shimmering beams of a full moon. And should this not happen, I will take comfort in recalling a bench that exists here on Earth beside a beloved school ... the bench which bears my name.

I do not regret being born to life as a Hill, and I hold no distress about the gradients I've traversed along the way ... the ones I conquered and those that conquered me. Like those on my walk this shining afternoon, the hills I've known have all been worth the climb.

APPENDIX

1924	Kermit and Violet born (Manhattan, Kansas and Kansas City, Missouri)
1937-1941	Kermit and Violet attend high school together in Kansas City
1944	Kermit and Violet marry in November, both twenty years old
1944-1946	Kermit sent overseas; Violet returns to Kansas City with her parents; Kermit returns to Kansas City after his tour of duty ends
1947	Kermit and Violet, twenty-three years old, settle in Washington, D.C. area Nancy born, in August, to the young couple
1947-1952	Family lives in Arlington VA; Kermit works as a White House Correspondent

1952	Family relocates to Kansas City, moves in with Violet's parents (the Robbs)
	Kermit seeks job in Kansas City or elsewhere
	Nancy goes to Kindergarten
1953-1957	Kermit secures job in Rochester, New York
	Family relocates to Rochester
	Nancy goes to Grades 1-4 (5?)
1957	Divorce occurs
1958	Kermit remains in Rochester
	Nancy and Violet move to Kansas City to live with Violet's parents (the Robbs)
1959-1965	Nancy and Violet move to nearby Raytown
	Nancy goes to junior and senior high school
1965	Nancy graduates from High School and enters the University of Missouri, Columbia
1968	Nancy and John marry
1969-1978	Nancy and John graduate from the University of Missouri, move to Kansas City
	Two sons born in 1974 and 1978
1978	Nancy, John and sons move to Pittsburgh, Pennsylvania

ACKNOWLEDGEMENTS

*F*aith, Friends, Family.

For fueling the writing of *Don't Fault the Moon*, I find myself—again the teacher—thanking not the three R's, but three F's.

FAITH: I think not of the traditional concept of faith, though certainly my trust in the Almighty has played a part. The Faith to which I refer is the all-important faith in oneself. Largely because of the other two F's, below, I gained faith in myself as a person, a memoirist, a writer. With this faith, I have cleared a huge hurdle in life.

FRIENDS: To the second of my three F's, I owe a debt of great gratitude. To my "old" friends, Linda Holley and Emilie Burr, I say thanks a million for reading, reflecting, and reacting—and also for reconnecting. Our renewed bonds enrich my life.

My dear Florida bookish buddies supported me

through the months, and years, of writing, revising, commiserating, and — finally — producing for their review my ragged first draft of *Don't Fault the Moon,* though it was called something different back then. Bless you, Jane Helsing, for alerting me to the initial writing workshop. And Coleen Oleski, Jane Helsing, Carol Durgin, Kay and Joel Sherard — your thoughts, reactions, and reorganizations were the keys to removing many weak elements from my draft. I thank Barbara Myers for providing a venue (many wonderful parties) for presenting pieces to an audience. And I send great gratitude and love to dear, now-departed Dee Zonarich for so many words of encouragement. Dee, my faith leads me to believe that if you could activate your famous "flying fingers" in their celestial setting, you would still have wisdom to impart.

Finally, thanks to my newly acquired literary friends and mentors who helped me plod along this sometimes-rocky path toward the vista of completion. Betty Jo Buro, you lit the bulb . . . and imparted the skills to keep it glowing. June O'Brien, your workshops and feedback brought so many long-ago-learned literary devices back to my psyche. Gina Hogan Edwards, writer, coach, and true professional, to you I owe a huge debt of gratitude for modeling excellence, endurance and inspiration. Melody A Scout and Penny Miller, BBRs (best beta readers) — thank you for the insightful fine-tuning which took the manuscript up another notch. Bobbie Lord, your unshakeable faith in my work has kept me going. Angie Dietrick–your patient readings, re-readings, insights and treasured discussions clarified my thinking. I send deep appreciation to Valerie Valentine for excellence in editing, empathy and most importantly for the very first professional endorsement of Nancy Hill, author. Your affirmation bolstered my faith in myself as a writer; your words meant the world. And finally, huge thanks to editor/publisher Alexa Nazzaro, for pushing me to go ever deeper and for, as her motto states, not letting me "publish crap." You are a tough taskmaster, Alexa, and I am a better writer for knowing you. Thanks also to your talented teammates — Tonia and Deividas.

FAMILY: I do not leave the least until last. My deepest gratitude goes to Alison Armstrong, sister/caring confidante/loving listener, and to cousins with comments Gary, Andrew and Tony. This author cherishes your input and our renewed connections.

To my sons, daughters-in-law, and grandchildren— while you witnessed in silence this flight of fancy of mine (praying that you would remain unidentifiable), your background love bolstered me each step of the way. And to precious Bentley, dearly departed, thank you for the patience and devotion in your big brown eyes and gently thumping tail as you suffered through interminable hours of clicking keys when what you really wanted to do was walk on the beach. You never complained and I miss you dearly.

I leave the best till last. To my husband and partner on fifty-seven years of this path, both in its living and its recollection, I owe everything. Memory jogger, fact-checker, in-house counsel, patient doer of laundry, shopper of groceries, and, yes, dog walker to the beach, uncomplaining and ever-faithful supporter, your confidence in me has sustained my traverse of dark tunnels and deep valleys to the peaks of this work and this life. Nothing good has ever been possible without John, and it is thanks to him that this daughter no longer faults the moon.

Faith, Friends, Family . . . and now, Readers. I am blessed.

About the Author

A lifetime lover of reading and writing, Nancy Hill became an author in 2021 with the publication of *Don't Fault the Moon*, a story she held in mind for decades before it became her memoir. An excerpt from *Don't Fault the Moon* was awarded third place in the Tallahassee Writers Association's 2020 Seven Hills Review Contest for Creative Non-fiction. Nancy and her husband live seasonally in Stuart, Florida, and Pittsburgh, Pennsylvania, where she spends her time writing, thinking about writing, reading about writing, talking about writing—or doing all of those while golfing, enjoying water activities, cherishing family and friends . . . and savoring the moon.

Made in the USA
Middletown, DE
06 June 2022

66757418R00146